Advanced Intelligent Predictive Models for Urban Transportation

Advanced Intelligent Predictive Models for Urban Transportation

R. Sathiyaraj, A. Bharathi and B. Balamurugan

CRC Press
Taylor & Francis Group
Boca Raton London New York

CRC Press is an imprint of the
Taylor & Francis Group, an **informa** business

A CHAPMAN & HALL BOOK

ISBN: 9781032108513 (hbk)
ISBN: 9781032228044 (pbk)
ISBN: 9781003217367 (ebk)

DOI: 10.1201/9781003217367

Typeset in Palatino
by Deanta Global Publishing Services, Chennai, India

Contents

Preface

The tremendous growth in transport systems and the increase in the number of vehicles on the roads in recent decades have created a significant problem in urban areas, namely traffic congestion. Traffic congestion inroads have been the biggest problem in the largest cities around the globe, especially cities in developing countries, where roads are not well designed and traffic on the roads is poorly managed. Traffic congestion increases fuel consumption and causes air pollution. In recent years, minimizing road traffic congestion has been a significant challenge; many researchers have focused on discovering the causes of traffic congestion. Some recent research works have merely identified the causes of traffic jams and suggest alternate routes to avoid traffic congestion. Besides, traffic forecasting requires accurate traffic models which can analyze the actual traffic condition statistically.

Intelligent transport systems (ITS) are being designed to develop the quality and sustainability of mobility by incorporating data as well as communication technologies with transport engineering. Other studies on ITS from the perspective of artificial intelligence (AI) have also been done. ITS depends on a capillary network of sensors which are installed on the roads to provide information on traffic variables like flow, speed, and density. These variables are monitored by administration centers to approximate traffic dynamics and apply control operations.

This book recommends a smart framework for the domain of transportation that performs traffic prediction with a fuel consumption model and analyzes traffic flow congestion using a genetic and regression model. It also proposes a traffic light controller and traffic deviation system based on a multi-agent system. First, this framework proposes a smart traffic prediction and congestion avoidance system based on the genetic model to reduce fuel consumption and pollution. The model uses Poisson distribution for the prediction of vehicle arrival based on recurring size. This model comprises traffic identification, prediction, and congestion avoidance phases. The system checks for the fitness function to determine traffic intensity and further uses predictive analytics to determine future traffic levels. It also integrates a fuel consumption model to save time and energy.

This framework then predicts short-term traffic flow using structure pattern and regression methods. Short-term traffic prediction is one of the required fields of study in the transportation domain. It is beneficial to develop a more advanced transportation system to control traffic signals and avoid congestion. The framework proposed will improve the traffic system and thereby also protect the environment, allowing rerouting, improving fuel consumption, and saving time. The traffic flow structure pattern can be constructed from freeway toll data. Based on the pattern, a prediction method was proposed, which is based on locally weighted learning (LWL) and regression.

Then this framework develops an efficient, intelligent traffic light control and deviation system for reducing traffic congestion to achieve a free flow of vehicles. Traffic light control systems are widely used to monitor and control the flow of automobiles through junctions on many roads. The intelligent traffic light control is critical for an efficient transportation system. This system is composed of a traffic light controller (TLC) and traffic light deviation (TLD). The TLC system uses three agents to supervise and control the traffic parameters. TLD system deviates the vehicles before entering into the congested road. The efficient intelligent traffic light control and deviation (EITLCD) system contains five elements: (i) Sensors: A magnetic sensor is chosen as a traffic sensor. (ii) Data collector agent:

This examines the data collected via the sensors, detect, count, and categorize the vehicles. (iii) Data processor agent: This determines vehicle length, velocity, and relative quantity of traffic. The data processor will manipulate the traffic data, and the input will be given to the intelligent traffic light controller (TLC) system. (iv) Intelligent TLC: This supervisor agent controls the traffic signal. This system has a threshold value depending on the traffic area, and if the value exists, then an alert signal will be sent to the deviation system. (v) Intelligent TDS: If a congestion state is predicted, the deviation system provides a signal to divert the vehicles arriving on the congested route.

An efficient smart intelligent transportation system (s-ITS) is made up of various components such as a central server, a radio frequency identification (RFID) device, sensors, a lighting control unit, and an EBOX II. The central server plays a significant role in providing resilience during any malfunctioning of the system. The RFID helps in communicating in data flow information between the cars and the EBOX II. This RFID device has tags and antennas to transmit information and readers to decode the data. It involves the smart building of the intelligent transport system with the ability to tackle real-time issues. The intelligent system is built to address the following modules: (i) Vehicular location tracking: This reduces the time required to select paths for the vehicles as well as providing easy location estimation. (ii) Intelligent vehicle parking system: Vehicle parking decisions are made based on outcome factors like whether a space is occupied or free. (iii) Communication within a VANET: The sensors track the location of the vehicle and its status in the current traffic scenario. (iv) Vehicular Big Data mining: Signals are communicated to the vehicles based on the mining of a huge volume of previous similar data and also on current traffic status.

It then operates traffic signals intelligently to enable emergency vehicles (ambulances) to move on without any inconvenience to commuters. The rapidly increasing vehicle population in India causes many issues in transport management for emergency vehicles such as ambulances, the fire service, and other emergency vehicles in the cities and towns of the country. Many patients are dead on arrival at hospital due to unforeseen traffic situations and inadequate responses from other road users compared with other countries. To minimize the traffic problems typically faced by ambulances, an intelligent transport system is proposed. It is integrated with sensor information and communication technologies to achieve traffic efficiency, thereby improving environmental quality, conserving energy, saving time, and enhancing safety and comfort, especially for ambulance drivers. The planned system has two modules which communicate and are controlled via sophisticated hardware components: An intelligent traffic light control system and an ambulance control system. The intelligent traffic light control system can ensure the current duration time and also give priority to some lanes according to real-time traffic conditions. The system can ease traffic jams by improving traffic management and effectively improving road use. The ambulance control system significantly solves ambulance problems like finding the fastest route for an ambulance. This system also determines those routes that are interrupted by congestion and other activities during peak hours and calculates the fastest route.

Authors

R. Sathiyaraj is an Assistant Professor in the School of Engineering & Technology at the CMR University, Bangalore, India. He obtained his Ph.D. in Computer Science and Engineering from Anna University, Chennai, India. He is a prominent researcher in the areas of Big Data analytics, machine learning, and the IoT and has published over 15 articles in various top international journals. He holds two authored books and one edited book.

A. Bharathi received her Bachelor's degree from Bharathiar University, Coimbatore, India and her postgraduate degree from Anna University, Chennai, India. She received her doctoral degree in Information and Communication Engineering, specializing in data mining, from Anna University, Chennai. She has over 22 years of teaching experience. She has published more than 85 research papers in reputed national and international journals, and presented more than 50 technical papers at international/national level conferences.

B. Balamurugan received his B.E. degree in Computer Science and Engineering from Bharathidasan University, Tiruchirappalli, India, in 2001, his M.E. degree in Computer Science and Engineering from Anna University, Chennai, India, in 2005, and his Ph.D. degree in Computer Science and Engineering from VIT University, Vellore, India, in 2015. He is currently a Professor with the School of Computing Science and Engineering, Galgotias University, Greater Noida, India. His current research interests include big data, network security, and cloud computing. He is a Pioneer Researcher in the areas of big data and the IoT and has published over 70 articles in various top international journals.

1

Overview

1.1 Introduction

With the rapid development of urban areas, the volume of vehicles has greatly increased, leading to issues such as collisions, traffic congestion, economic losses, environmental pollution, and excessive fuel waste. Among these issues, road traffic jams represent a significant problem related to the field of urban transportation. Intelligent transportation systems (ITS) is an interdisciplinary field that uses data analytics from different mathematical models, and is also seen as an important technology for alleviating congestion in urban traffic. Accurate traffic forecasting and traffic light regulation are important steps in the development of an ITS and are essential for transport system efficiency.

An efficient traffic management system is needed to forecast and control traffic flows in urban areas. Prediction of traffic helps to avoid traffic congestion before it develops. Typically, urban traffic forecasting uses historical and current traffic flow data to predict future road conditions (Niu *et al.* 2015). With the development of smart phone technology, sensors are widely used to analyze traffic conditions. For managing and forecasting traffic congestion, machine learning algorithms and Big Data analytics techniques are used. Big Data analytics plays an essential role in the intelligent traffic management system reach. Data analytics helps us to predict traffic congestion, and its occurrence can be avoided.

This book recommends a smart framework for the domain of transportation that performs traffic prediction with a fuel consumption model and analyzes traffic flow congestion using a genetic and regression model. Based on a multi-agent system, it will control traffic lights and deviate traffic routes.

1.2 Towards Intelligent Traffic Flow Prediction

Road traffic congestion is a persistent problem worldwide. With the huge growth of the population, the number of vehicles is increasing at a rapid rate. India is the second largest country in terms of growth in population and economy. Most cities in India are facing road congestion problems. There are practical difficulties in maintaining intelligent transport management systems (ITMS) in metropolitan cities in India. This is due to the slow growth in infrastructure compared to the rapid increase in the number of vehicles, as well as space and cost constraints.

Traffic flow information is needed to help travelers to make better travel decisions when it comes to congestion and to improve traffic operation efficiency. Predicting short-term traffic flow will be more helpful in managing freeway networks. This traffic flow prediction makes use of real-time data to predict traffic status in the subsequent 5–20 minutes. Every country in the world is striving to enhance their traffic management systems to make them more efficient. Researchers have used different methods to predict freeway traffic in urban areas.

1.3 Broad Factors Impacting Traffic Flow

Traffic congestion on the road can be defined as the condition in which the number of vehicles in the lane is higher than the lane capacity. Traffic congestion may occur due to various reasons. The primary reason may vary depending on the location. It occurs when the demand exceeds road capacity. Reasons for traffic congestion include an increased number of vehicles in the lane, improper parking, road maintenance work, accidents, etc.

Traffic congestion has a wide range of consequences, including squandering time for users and causing delays in reaching their destinations, increased fuel consumption, pollution, and a higher risk of collisions, among others. This is a serious issue which needs to be dealt with. Solutions for the problem need to be developed. Some possible solutions are parking restrictions, changes in school timings to reduce rush hours, traffic counters, better traffic management, speed limit enforcement, lane splitting, provision of flyovers, construction of metro systems, public education programs, etc.

To reduce traffic congestion, a novel traffic flow management model is needed. In this book, the focus is to develop a model which can eliminate traffic congestion, thereby resulting in a uniform flow of traffic. The causes and effects of traffic congestion and the most appropriate solutions to the problem vary according to the location.

1.4 Prediction Techniques on Traffic Flow

With the advent of information and communication technologies, many traffic forecasting models have been developed to help traffic management and control. This section discusses work related to traffic analysis, prediction, congestion, and traffic light control.

To predict traffic flow, a novel approach based on long short-term memory (LSTM) (Ma *et al.* 2015) has been suggested. Lin *et al.* (2017) propose a novel fuzzy deep-learning approach called FDCN to predict the citywide flow of traffic. This method is based on the theory of fuzzy logic and the model of the deep residual network. Do *et al.* (2019) propose a deep learning–based traffic flow predictor with spatial and temporal attentions (STANN).

To establish the spatial dependencies between road segments and temporal dependencies between time steps, spatial and temporal attention is deployed (Hou et al. 2019) – an adaptive hybrid model to predict the short-term flow of traffic. To predict traffic flow, the linear autoregressive integrated moving average (ARIMA) and non-linear wavelet neural network (WNN) method was used. The outputs of the two individual models were then evaluated and combined by fuzzy logic, and the weighted result was regarded as the final predicted traffic volume of the hybrid model.

Atta *et al.* (2018) proposed an intelligent system which maintains the active timings of traffic signals by sensing traffic density and reducing overcrowding with IoT (Internet of Things) sensors, which offer powerful and advanced communication technology. A new model by Zaki *et al.* (2019), based on hidden Markov model and contrast, defines traffic states during peak hours in two-dimensional space (2D). This model uses mean speed and contrasts to capture the variability in traffic patterns.

1.5 Generic Traffic Flow Prediction Models and Measurements

Existing research on traffic flow forecasting primarily focused on reducing traffic congestion and providing uninterrupted traffic flow.A large number of research studies are focused on traffic forecasting, with the majority of models focusing on short-term traffic forecasting. Approaches are normally categorized as either parametric or nonparametric (Van Lint *et al.* 2002) (Vlahogianni & Karlaftis 2013).

These approaches mainly focus on the structure of the model and real-time traffic scenarios. To improve the accuracy of prediction, ARIMA (Williams & Hoel 2003) and STARIMA approaches (Pfeifer & Deutsch 1980) were proposed.

Several data mining and machine learning methods are employed in predicting traffic. These approaches are the classification trees model (CTM) (Kim *et al.* 2008) (Zhan *et al.* 2011), decision trees (DT), artificial neural networks (ANN) (Wei & Lee 2007) (Vlahogianni & Karlaftis 2013), genetic algorithms (GA) (Valenti *et al.* 2010), and support/relevance vector machines (SVM/RVM) (Luo *et al.* 2019).

Intelligent transportation systems (ITS) are indispensable in proposing solutions to these types of problems. However, the abrupt volume of vehicles involved in urban transportation necessitates the use of Big Data analytics to process information and utilize traffic systems in an optimized way (Vlahogianni *et al.*2008). Regression techniques are proposed to model vehicle arrivals based on real-time data (Lippi *et al.* 2013). Accurate traffic prediction (Liu *et al.* 2016) is proposed as a traffic estimation method which makes use of road network correlation and sparse traffic sampling.

Time-series is the major factor in almost any of the traffic flow prediction models. A local linear regression model was used in short-term traffic forecasting (Sun *et al.* 2004). In the same traffic flow forecasting, a Bayesian network approach was employed (Sun, *et al.* 2006) to predict short-term traffic flow, and a support vector–based online learning weighted support vector regression approach was proposed (Jeong *et al.* 2013). Many researchers have focused on providing an efficient solution for traffic management and control. The focus was turned on machine learning techniques, which provided a path for academics and industries to focus their attention on smart intelligent transport management systems (SITMS).

A prediction methodology based on deep learning was proposed (Lv *et al.* 2014) for analyzing the system. A stacked auto encoder model was employed in a greedy layer-wise fashion. An approach for forecasting travel speed for multi-step-ahead based on 2-min travel speed data using fuzzy neural networks was proposed (Tang *et al.* 2017).

Chiu and Chand (1993) have proposed an approach adapting the fixed type controller approach. These have been programmed to function at preset timings for each series. This solution was used for various types of traffic scenarios and especially for undisciplined traffic. Several research techniques have attempted to avoid using a fixed cycle controller system, but ITS still requires a cost-effective method for reducing traffic congestion.

Addressing a single issue may not be an efficient solution; several parameters have to be considered to avoid traffic congestion in advance. Vehicle speed and length are considered the two most important factors in any traffic management system.

VANET is a technology that considers vehicles as nodes in a network and creates a mobile network for data exchange and communication, whereby each vehicle will participate in exchanging information related to traffic conditions. VANETs provide better techniques to collect real-time traffic related information in a cost effective manner and traffic information delivery (Hartenstein & Laberteaux 2009). V2V and V2R communications in VANETs help to gather traffic updates from vehicles and roadside units.

To gather real-time traffic related data, many techniques rely on loop and mobile detectors. Because cellular phones are not dedicated to traffic data swap, this type of detection is costly and results in huge amounts of traffic information. The cost of implementing the loop detector systems is very high (Wang *et al.* 2014). Delays in communication and the degradation of safety result in an incompetent system. Timing and security issues in ITS with VANETs are addressed (Zheng *et al.* 2017).

An efficient traffic light system is proposed by Shandiz *et al.* (2009) which uses a genetic algorithm to evaluate the stochastic data, thereby arriving at an optimized transport system. The data is compiled, each traffic signal is coded, and then the data is analysed collectively for each path to determine the ideal condition. The imitation is completed using the length of the route and average vehicle speed.

The research helps to determine the conditions in which the maximum number of vehicles can go through the traffic lights. The concurrent examination of a lot of objects with a number of statistical measures is provided through a multivariate study (Hair, William, Barry & Rolphe 2010). Using this method, a concurrent study is carried out on the above two variables. Different multivariate study techniques have been proposed that could be applied as per the requirement.

Petracca *et al.* (2013) propose a prototype for a vehicle which is capable of interacting with other roadside vehicles and also with an internal electronic device. The model also specifies the different mechanisms in the on-board element. This offers a variety of applications that could be used to develop well-organized operations.

This study (Hair, William, Barry & Rolphe 2010) (Hair *et al.* 1998) gives an overview of the various requirements for designing an efficient ITS system. Simulations are completed using MATLAB to establish the accuracy of the proposed scheme based on real-world circumstances. The observations show that the proposed environment helps in identifying vehicle positions in different environments.

The algorithm is examined in terms of running time and result accuracy. (De la Garza *et al.*2013) propose novel schemes which integrate IoT with the intelligent transportation scheme so as to improve transportation.

1.6 Motivation

Traffic congestion is a significant problem, especially in growing nations; to counter this, many models for traffic systems have been proposed. For smart transportation systems, a new framework is traffic prediction, which is needed to avoid congestion. This proposes a smart framework for the domain of transportation that performs traffic prediction with a fuel consumption model and analyzes traffic flow congestion using genetic and regression models. It also proposes a traffic light controller with a traffic deviation system using a multi-agent system.

The sample data is taken on an hourly volume in the low and moderate ranges, and a probability model and genetic prediction model for predicting traffic congestion and avoidance are established. The use of this prediction technique with a fuel consumption model helps to avoid congestion and also reduces pollution, protecting the green environment and ensuring safe traveling conditions.

1.7 Problem Statement and Research Objective

1.7.1 Problem Statement

The tremendous growth in transport systems and the increase in the number of vehicles over the last decades have created a significant problem in urban areas, namely traffic congestion. Traffic congestion increases fuel consumption and causes air pollution. By answering the following research questions, this research aims to solve these problems:

- How to predict and avoid road traffic congestion;
- How to predict the traffic flow pattern and what method should be used to do this;
- How to control traffic lights and how to implement deviation systems;
- How to develop an intelligent transportation system for controlling traffic.

1.7.2 Research Objectives

- To propose traffic prediction and congestion avoidance based on a genetic model to reduce fuel consumption and pollution;
- To predict short-term traffic flow using structure pattern and regression methods; using the pattern information and locally weighted learning (LWL), to predict the traffic flow in a week;
- To develop an efficient, intelligent traffic light control and deviation system for reducing traffic congestion and achieve free flow of vehicles;
- To propose an IoT-based intelligent transportation system for providing smart traffic solutions for the smart city;
- To operate traffic signals intelligently to enable emergency vehicles (ambulances) to travel without any inconvenience to commuters.

1.8 Outline of the Book

The organization of the book is as follows.

In Chapter 2, a comprehensive survey of various traffic flow prediction methods is presented. The chapter elucidates the details of the implications of these methods while applying traffic analysis, prediction, and congestion and traffic light controller concepts in traffic flow prediction assessment procedures.

A smart traffic prediction and congestion avoidance system (S-TPCA) using genetic predictive models for urban transportation is implemented and illustrated in Chapter 3. This chapter proposes predicting traffic congestion based on the arrival time of vehicles, thereby helping to reduce traffic congestion before it occurs. This chapter examines the performance efficiency of the proposed algorithms by evaluating the results concerning arrival time and fuel consumption.

Chapter 4 describes short-term traffic prediction, which is one of the required fields of study in the transportation domain. It is beneficial to develop a more advanced transportation system to control traffic signals and avoid congestion. The proposed short-term traffic flow prediction is based on structure pattern and regression methods. The experiment examines the performance efficiency of the proposed algorithm by evaluating the results concerning minimum and maximum traffic during weekends and holidays with an RMSE (root mean squared error) method.

A novel framework is reported in Chapter 5 that illustrates an efficient, intelligent traffic light control and deviation (EITLCD) system based on the multi-agent system. It is composed of traffic light control (TLC) and traffic light deviation (TLD). The performance evaluation of the proposed system with the various related systems in terms of pro-activeness, adaptability, performance, time, and cost are considered for comparison with multiple approaches.

In Chapter 6, an IoT-based intelligent transportation system (IoT-ITS) is proposed and discussed from a global perspective. It assists in mechanizing railways, airways, roadways, and marine traffic, improving the experience of customers regarding the way in which merchandise is transferred, monitored, and transported. The performance of the model is studied and deliberations are reported.

Chapter 7 describes an intelligent traffic light control system and ambulance control system. It is integrated with sensor information and communication technologies to achieve traffic efficiency, improve environmental quality, save energy and time, and enhance safety and comfort, especially for ambulance drivers. The performance of the model is studied and deliberations are reported.

Conclusions and the potential for future enhancement are described in Chapter 8.

2

Related Works

2.1 Introduction

Most cities are experiencing a major growth in population and face many challenges as they expand at an increasing rate. Traffic is one of the most challenging issues in all developing cities.

Table 2.1 shows the measures taken by some highly regarded cities in controlling traffic. Traffic congestion is one of the major challenges in enabling urbanization. The deployment of intelligent transportation systems (ITS) in urban areas brings opportunities to prevent or reduce traffic congestion.

2.2 Traffic Flow Prediction

In recent decades, various traffic prediction models have been created to help traffic control and administration for improving transportation, ranging from path direction and vehicle navigation to signal coordination. The issue of traffic flow prediction can be explained as follows: Let X_{it} denote the observed traffic flow quantity during the tth time interval at the ith observation location in a transportation network. Given a sequence $\{X_{it}\}$ of observed traffic flow data, $i = 1, 2..., m, t = 1, 2..., T$, the problem is to predict the traffic flow at a time distance $(t + \Delta)$ for forecast horizon Δ. Researchers have explored many techniques to forecast traffic volume, and Table 2.2 presents essential strategies in the territory of traffic flow analysis and traffic flow prediction, showing their advantages and disadvantages.

Early research in traffic predictions used different techniques. Okutani and Stephanedes (1984) proposed applying Kalman filtering with two different models to estimate traffic count. Historical traffic data is more commonly used in some prediction models (Migliavacca & Cugola 2007), while others rely on real-time traffic information (Habtemichael & Cetin 2016). For example, Rice and Van Zwet (2004) used the Random Walk Forest (Williams & Hoel 2003) method for current traffic situations to predict traffic flow. Conversely, a technique like the autoregressive integrated moving average (ARIMA) procedure (Barimani et al. 2014) reveals the short-term traffic situations in a particular road network based on the preceding traffic flow in a specified area. The inputs in the main predictive models are historical or real-time data, but Chrobok et al. (2001) emphasized merging both types of data to enhance the final prediction result.

Rice and Van Zwet (2004) integrated historical data and real-time data for forecasting. More attention has been given to research traffic valuation and forecasting. However, the restrictions of those models remain. For example, transportation systems might be affected

DOI: 10.1201/9781003217367-2

TABLE 2.1

Traffic Measures

S. No.	Name of the City	Measure
1.	Stockholm	Electronic road pricing
2.	Barcelona	Urban Lab – dynamic traffic forecasting
3.	London	Electronic journey planner
4.	Hong Kong	Public light bus
5.	Copenhagen	Integrative public transport model
6.	Hangzhou	Public cycling system
7.	United Kingdom	Active traffic management approach

by factors such as accidents and weather (Pan *et al.* 2018). In particular, extreme weather circumstances may have a severe impact on traffic flow and travel time (Koesdwiady *et al.* 2016).

Khandelwal *et al.* (2015) applied fuzzy logic to calculate the influence of social factors on stock price prediction. The proposed method can be used to examine the external factors that affect traffic count data on the road using fuzzy logic. Snow, rain, fog, the period of day, the geographical location of a place, planned or unplanned road construction, and accidents can all influence traffic data and complicate the prediction process. We can compare relevant factors of real-time data (forecasting data) with corresponding factors of historical data by preserving those seven patterns in traffic data, and only a matching set of data should be chosen for future prediction (Zadeh 1965).

A concept of fuzzy logic as a method of processing data can be explained by discussing partial set membership as opposed to crisp set membership. The principal strategies of the parametric approach are based on ARIMA models (Williams & Hoel 2003) and Kalman filtering (Barimani *et al.* 2014). Traffic flow has a stochastic and nonlinear nature, but these models predict traffic without considering these characteristics which leads to a substantial error in the prediction. In the second approach, a nonparametric regression (Yoon & Chang 2014) is generally utilized procedure.

Zheng and Su (2014) used a k nearest neighbor nonparametric regression model for short-term traffic prediction. Liu and Wang (2016) proposed support vector regression to establish the network traffic prediction model, whereas the global artificial fish swarm algorithm (GAFSA) was used to optimize the model's parameters. Artificial neural networks (ANNs) were proposed to predict traffic flow. Unfortunately, the problem of local minima still exists in ANNs appropriate procedures. Moreover, ANNs almost always use a single hidden layer. Simulations have shown that one hidden layer is insufficient to illustrate the complicated relationship between data sources and forecast model yields. Hybrid approaches have been explored by some researchers to deal with the obdurate nature of time series in nonparametric models. These methodologies are more flexible while consolidating different events.

In recent times, numerous prediction models have brought together the thinking of researchers in numerous areas, particularly in time series prediction. Khandelwal *et al.* (2015) used a combination of DWT, ANN, and ARIMA where experiments are performed on four different time series. Also, the inspiration for using DWT to partition linearity and nonlinearity is taken from (Zhang, GP 2003), founded by Zhang, who pointed out that time series data contains both linear and nonlinear patterns. The same approach is taken in Wang, Y *et al.* (2017), which discusses the usage of the piecewise method ARIMA model and the SVM model to perform short-term traffic flow prediction.

To predict travel speed for multi-step-ahead, Zheng and Su (2014) built a fuzzy neural network using 2-minute travel speed data. Tang *et al.* (2018) projected the use of adaptive

TABLE 2.2

Review of Prediction Methods

Title	Author	Year	Advantages	Disadvantages
Traffic flow prediction using neural network	Jiber, M, Lamouik, I, Ali, Y & Sabri	2018	Deep learning architecture to predict road traffic flow with the ability to reconstruct lost or destroyed data with the predicted values.	Unexpected conditions such as events, holidays, and accidents might affect the accuracy.
Short-term traffic speed prediction for an urban corridor	Yao, B, Chen, C, Cao, Q, Jin, L, Zhang, M, Zhu, H & Yu, B	2017	Support vector machine model–based short-term prediction with spatial-temporal parameters using high accuracy.	Prediction model is single-step; when the traffic speed is higher than 35 km/h, the prediction accuracy is reduced.
Traffic flow prediction using Kalman filtering technique	Kumar, SV	2017	Uses real-time as well as historical (2 days' worth) data for prediction.	Nothing has been done for missing values.
Traffic flow forecasting using time series decomposition model in urban midblock sections	Omkar, G & Kumar	2017	Compares to ARIMA; multiplicative decomposition technique is used which needs a smaller amount of data. Both real-time and historical data are used.	External factors and missing data are not considered, such as accidents and weather.
Weather information based improving traffic flow prediction in connected cars: A deep learning approach	Koesdwiady, A, Soua, R & Karray	2016	Study of traffic flow prediction with the effect of weather data using deep belief networks	High usage of memory for the training process.
Big Data based traffic flow prediction: A deep learning approach	Lv, Y, Duan, Y, Kang, W, Li, Z & Wang	2014	Examines historical and real-time data to be inputted in a greedy approach which provides fantastic performance.	Takes a lot of time, and the data used are produced synthetically.
Real-time traffic flow predicting using augmented reality	Zhang, M	2016	Provides superior accuracy.	Data used to forecast is made synthetically; it does not consider chaotic situations.
Seasonal ARIMA model based short-term traffic flow prediction with input data limitation	Kumar, SV & Vanajakshi	2015	Overcomes issue of the sound database for ARIMA model by using the past 3 days' worth of data.	It uses the past 3 days' worth of data but it might not take into account weekly or monthly patterns, which can be useful information in traffic prediction.
Multi-step prediction of Volterra neural network for traffic flow based on chaos algorithm	Yin, L, He, Y, Dong, X & Lu, Z	2012	Considers both historical and real-time data for long-term prediction.	Takes too much time as it considers many data.

fuzzy neural network (AFFN) to develop a lane-changing predictor to predict steering angles. To enhance the accuracy of prediction, an approach to using the distinctive strengths of DWT, ARIMA, and ANN was proposed. Fuzzy logic and DWT was used to enhance the accuracy of traffic-flow forecasting based on hourly data. A lot of research is being performed merging two or more techniques to forecast traffic flow.

Obviously, Khandelwal *et al.* (2015) recommended that neither ANN nor ARIMA is generally appropriate for all types of time series. Every real-world time series contains both nonlinear and linear correlation structures among the annotations. Zhang (2003) has pointed out this important fact and has developed a hybrid approach that applies ARIMA and ANN separately for modeling the linear and nonlinear components of a time series. Furthermore, (Khandelwal *et al.* 2015) specified a novel hybrid approach which has utilized DWT to change the nonlinear and linear components of the time series. The proposed technique will have the benefit of changing time series information into linear time-series information. Further, it will be used in the final ARIMA forecasting model to predict the result.

Figure 2.1 categorizes studies on traffic flow prediction into two categories: 1) parametric approaches and 2) nonparametric approaches.

2.2.1 Parametric Approaches

In the early stage of traffic flow prediction, parametric approaches were typically proposed. Parametric methods are usually based on the assumption of specific functions for some variables (either independent or dependent). These approaches include the autoregressive integrated moving average (ARIMA) model (Van Der Voort *et al.* 1996), Holt Winter (Grubb & Mason 2001), and their variants (Williams & Hoel 2003). These linear time-series models can determine the trend and periodicity information from the flow.

The advantages of these linear time series models include simplicity and efficiency, while the main disadvantage is the low accuracy due to the impact of the chaotic and fractal characteristics of traffic flow. Other models have been proposed to improve the prediction accuracy of traffic flow. A method of integrating the Kalman filter and ARIMA model was proposed by Stathopoulos and Karlaftis (2003). Experimental results also verify the effectiveness of the proposed method.

The benefit of the Kalman filter is to update the state variables continuously so that it can improve prediction accuracy (Okutani & Stephanedes 1984). Moreover, Nair *et al.* (2001) established a nonlinear time series model to analyze traffic data. Furthermore,

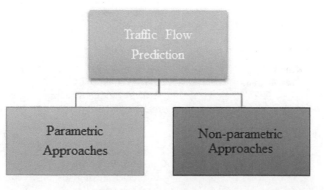

FIGURE 2.1
Traffic flow prediction categories.

Vlahogianni *et al.* (2008) present a multilayer strategy to identify and cluster nonlinear traffic structural patterns.

2.2.2 Nonparametric Approaches

The proliferation of various sensors deployed in ITS results in the availability of massive amounts of traffic data. Nonparametric (or data-driven) approaches based on such traffic data can potentially improve traffic flow prediction. In general, machine learning (ML)–based methods can identify the patterns and capture the key features of traffic flows, consequently improving prediction accuracy. In Yu *et al.* (2016), a short-term traffic condition prediction model based on a k-nearest neighbor algorithm was proposed.

The study by Ko *et al.* (2016) proposed a Markov process–based method to predict traffic conditions between roads. Among ML-based methods, an artificial neural network (ANN) can accurately recognize the traffic patterns, consequently surpassing other ML methods (Smith & Demetsky 1994). Typically, an ANN needs to update the weights of the hidden layer via back propagation (Buscema 1998). Such ANN methods are called back-propagation neural networks (BPNN).

Many BPNN-based or hybrid BPNN-based models (2008) have been proposed in traffic flow prediction. Deep learning (DL) models have the advantage of being able to process the intricate and hierarchical aspects of vast data when compared to traditional BPNN-based methods (Mohamed *et al.* 2011). Recently, DL methods have shown their strengths in traffic flow prediction (Huang, W *et al.* 2014), driving behavior feature extraction (Liu *et al.* 2017), and city-wide crowd flow prediction (Zheng *et al.* 2017).

One DL model is the recurrent neural network (RNN), which has the advantage of capturing time-series characteristics during the training and predicting phase (Van Lint *et al.* 2002). Long short-term memory (LSTM) (Hochreiter & Schmidhuber 1997) improves RNN by including memory cells which can preserve information for a long period. As a result, LSTM can learn longer-term dependencies. Recently, both RNN and LSTM models have been investigated in travel speed prediction (Ma *et al.* 2015) and short-term traffic flow forecasting (Zhao *et al.* 2017).

In addition, convolution neural networks (CNN) have also been used in transportation network speed prediction (Ma *et al.* 2017). Moreover, many other factors such as weather conditions and special events have an influence on traffic flow. In particular, weather conditions (such as rainfall and snow) (Tang *et al.* 2017) can affect the urban traffic flow. For example, rainfall intensity and visibility can significantly affect freeway traffic flow.

Moreover, Yi *et al.* (2017) show that rainfall intensity may alter users' route choice, consequently affecting traffic flow. In addition to weather conditions, special events or accident events can also significantly affect traffic flow. For example, traffic flow fluctuates differently on the day of a special event day (like a football game) compared with an ordinary day. Moreover, an accident event like a traffic jam or an accident has a significant impact on traffic flow (Lin *et al.* 2017).

2.3 Traffic Incident Detection

Detection of incidents, congestion, and other traffic operational problems is very important for the operation of the traffic system. Intelligent classification methods can offer efficient ways to classify the state of the transport system.

Yeh *et al.* (2000) have applied a fuzzy multicriteria analysis to the performance evaluation of urban public transport systems. The fuzzy multicriteria analysis provides crisp ranking outcomes for the evaluation problem. An empirical study of ten bus companies in Taipei's public transport system has been carried out to exemplify the approach.

Wen *et al.* (2001) have developed a probabilistic neural network to solve the problem of incident detection. Efficient incident management is an important issue in freeway traffic management systems. A broad variety of events that contain various patterns during a range of traffic periods and flow conditions were used to train and assess the performance accuracy and the transfer capability of the algorithm based on a probabilistic neural network. Test results with simulation data showed that the probabilistic neural network has the potential to achieve good incident detection performance.

For real-time traffic incident detection, Xu *et al.* (1998) developed a real-time online adaptive algorithm. The method consists of two stages. First, a real-time adaptive online process is utilized to determine the important traffic state mechanism, namely, the density and average velocity of the moving vehicles. Second, a neural network called fuzzy CMAC (cerebellar arithmetic computer) is applied to identify traffic incidents. CMAC consists of both a fuzzy logic unit and a neural network unit. The system will help drivers to select an optimum route, it will be able to provide information for efficient dispatching of emergency services and moreover, it will provide accurate knowledge of existing traffic conditions.

Lee *et al.* (1998) implemented an incident detection algorithm based on fuzzy logic that feeds an incident's details (i.e., the location, incident severity, and time) into the system's manager of optimization, which employs that data to verify a suitable plan of signal control. The developed algorithm was tested under laboratory conditions, and its overall performance was encouraging in terms of detection rate, false alarm rate, and mean time to detect. Fuzzy logic has been successfully used to detect traffic anomalies.

Weil *et al.* (1998) developed a novel time-indexed traffic anomaly detection algorithm. Depending on the type of the day and time of the day, the fuzzy sets "normal" and "abnormal" are determined for each traffic descriptor by using an unsupervised learning algorithm. Fusion of the multiple traffic descriptors, on a per lane basis, in order to determine membership of the "normal" or "abnormal" lane status is implemented with fuzzy composition techniques. Finally, each lane status is fused to determine an overall road segment status. Because of the significant difference in terms of performance, weight, and size between short vehicles (SVs) and long vehicles (LVs), vehicle classification data based on length are of basic significance for pavement design, traffic processes, and planning transportation.

The Highway Capacity Manual requires adjustments to heavy-vehicle volumes in capacity analysis. The roadway geometric design, such as curb heights and horizontal alignment, is impacted by the various moving characteristics of LVs because of their lesser braking, heavy weight, and huge turning radius. The heavy weight of such vehicles is also significant in pavement maintenance and design, as truck volumes influence both the design parameters and life of pavements. Safety is impacted by LVs: of serious vehicle-to-vehicle crashes, 8% concerned huge trucks, although they only accounted for 3% of all registered vehicles and 7% of all vehicle miles traveled (VMT). Recent studies also found that particulate matters (PM) are strongly associated with the onset of myocardial infarction and respiratory symptoms. Heavy-duty trucks that use diesel engines are major sources of PM, accounting for 72% of traffic emitted PM.

Traffic control is one of the fast growing areas among transport management problems. More efficient methods are needed for optimizing road capacity and traffic control systems. Traffic control involves different kinds of problems, for instance, traffic signal and light control, traffic assignment problems, scheduling and planning problems, and so on. Traffic-light control systems and intersection management systems seem to be the main issues in this problem area. Intelligent techniques as a part of decision-making can be very effective.

Fay and Schnieder (1999) have developed a dispatching support system for use in railway operation control systems. The system contains expert knowledge in fuzzy rules of the "IF–THEN" type. Actually, the system is a fuzzy Petri net notion that combines the graphical power of Petri nets and the capability of fuzzy sets to model rule-based expert knowledge in a decision support system. The proposed assistant system for dispatching support can be integrated into an operating center. Improvements can be seen in traffic performance, reliability, and customer satisfaction.

Correspondingly, Hegyi *et al.* (2001) have presented a fuzzy decision support system (FDSS) for assisting the operators of traffic control systems. The fuzzy decision support system is part of a larger traffic support system and it can be used to provide a limited list of appropriate combinations of traffic control measures for a given traffic situation. The main role of the fuzzy decision support system is to suggest whether a particular local traffic controller or control measure should be activated or not. The kernel of the system is a fuzzy case-base that is constructed using simulated scenarios. The FDSS uses a case-base and a fuzzy interpolation to generate a ranked listing of combinations of control measures and their estimated performance. In the future, this system will be complemented with an adaptive learning feature and with a set of fuzzy rules that incorporate the heuristic knowledge of experienced traffic operators. The fuzzy decision support system is very useful because a lot of knowledge concerning decision making in real situations is uncertain.

That was kept in mind when Aziz *et al.* (1999) developed a new strategy for aiding decision-making based on fuzzy inferences in the traffic regulation of an urban bus network. The system helps the operators of the urban bus network to solve the problem of connections between buses.

Sadek *et al.* (1999) examined the potential of using case-based reasoning (CBR), an emerging artificial intelligence paradigm, to overcome this problem. In their study, a prototype CBR routing system for an interstate network in Hampton Roads, Virginia, was developed. Cases for building the system's case-base were generated using heuristic dynamic traffic assignment (DTA) model designed for the region. The results showed that the prototype system is capable of running in real time, and of producing high quality solutions using case-bases of reasonable size.

Montero *et al.* (1998) have developed a combined methodology for transportation planning assessment. The methodology is a combination of a well-known traffic assignment tool, the EMME/2 model, with a microscopic traffic simulator, the Advanced Interactive Microscopic Simulator for Urban and Non-Urban Networks (AIMSUN2), with an emphasis on the description of the specific interfaces that make consistent the combination of both tools in a generic environment for traffic analysis and modeling (GETRAM) environment. The GETRAM environment has an open and flexible computer architecture suitable for modeling complex transportation systems. Evolutionary algorithms seemed to achieve some success as a planning tool for different kinds of networks.

2.4 Smart Traffic Prediction and Congestion Avoidance System

Reducing traffic congestion and providing uninterrupted traffic flow is the major goal behind smart traffic management systems. In India, many of the metropolitan cities are

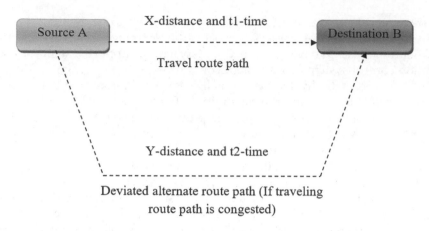

FIGURE 2.2
Congestion avoidance assumption.

facing difficulties in managing traffic since the rules are not strictly enforced and some of our traffic system rules were not in line with the current traffic situation.. This section focuses on providing a smart traffic system suitable for Asian continents. Prediction of traffic flow to avoid traffic congestion is one of the complicated problems in transportation planning and car navigation systems.

Smart traffic prediction and congestion avoidance systems can be used in particular areas that allow route deviation. Instead of constructing new roads to reduce traffic congestion, vehicles can be diverted to avoid congestion, and this also has several benefits for travelers, like reducing fuel consumption, saving money and time, and maintaining a green environment.

Figure 2.2 shows an assumption of congestion avoidance. If a vehicle is traveling from A to B, it requires a time, t1 (x is said to be the distance from A to B). If there is any traffic congestion on the route, then the traveling time of the vehicle will be increased – say t1+ μ is the time taken to reach the destination B (where μ will represent the time delay). When the vehicle is diverted, then the vehicle takes t2 time to get from A to B (a deviating signal is used to divert the vehicles). This deviated alternate route path may be slightly longer than the regular route, so the speed of the vehicle can be increased and the vehicle will not encounter traffic congestion. This will help it to reach its destination quickly and also results in a relaxed travel experience.

In the past, control measures aimed to minimize delay for all vehicles using the road system. With increasing concern for green/environmental issues, a range of objective functions must be put forward:

- Minimize overall delay to vehicles
- Minimize delays to public transport
- Minimize delays to emergency services
- Minimize delays to pedestrians
- Equitable distribution of delays between competing traffic
- Maximize reliability, i.e. minimize unpredictable variations in journey time for vehicle users
- Maximize network capacity to minimize accident potential for all users

- Minimize environmental impact of vehicular traffic (noise, atmospheric pollution, visual intrusion)
- Maximize energy efficiency

2.4.1 Approaches to Congestion Control

At present, most signal control methods aim to ease or prevent congestion. There are a few papers which deal directly with queue management in overloaded conditions. These schemes can be categorized into three main groups:

1) Capacity improvements: critical queues can be reduced by eliminating or relocating bottlenecks.
2) Queue regulation: traffic input to the tail of the critical queue can be regulated in order to control the queue length.
3) Restricting traffic input area-wide: traffic entering a busy area can be metered or restrained so as to reduce the probability of critical queue formation anywhere in the area.

Road widening schemes and junction improvements can remove bottlenecks and therefore decrease significant queue lengths. However, these procedures are costly and not always possible. Many bottlenecks are associated not so much with the physical layout of the road network, but with pedestrian and commercial activities which spill onto the carriageway. Measures for parking control, loading, and pedestrian crossing movements are applied repeatedly, but they are frequently not convenient to other users.

Improvements have been made through efficient traffic signal control methods. These have advantages over other capacity measures in that they are flexible and cheap and cause fewer disturbances to the urban fabric. Reconfiguring the traffic routing pattern within a city can increase capacity. For example, a one-way system can redistribute conflict and exploit unused stop-line capacity on adjacent streets.

Any capacity expansion strategy will promote further traffic growth. Therefore, it may delay the trouble – while still minimizing it – rather than offering a long-term solution. Queue control measures, on the other hand, involve regulating input as opposed to boosting output (although they may have the effect of increasing the capacity of the network by minimizing interference). By decreasing serious queue length and hence regulating the arrival rate, one can efficiently shift it to a fresh site, one selected to reduce the chance of queue propagation or restrict its spread. Calculations in the third major group use the similar common principle as the second; the distinction is that they are applied on an area-wide scale.

The main justification for restraint is that it frees up road space for other purposes, or contributes in some other way to wider objectives such as safety, urban conservation, or environmental quality. Further to these three groups, measures can be classified as either "static" (pre-planned) or "dynamic" in operational terms.

A huge number of research projects focus on traffic prediction, and most models focus on short-term traffic prediction. Approaches are normally categorized as parametric or nonparametric (Van Lint *et al.* 2002). These approaches focus mainly on the structure of the model and real-time traffic scenarios. To improve the accuracy of prediction, the ARIMA (Williams & Hoel 2003) and STARIMA (Pfeifer & Deutsch 1980) approaches were proposed. Several nonparametric approaches have been proposed with various advantages;

these approaches encompass Kalman filters (Guo *et al.* 2014), SVM (Liu, X *et al.* 2011), NNs (Karlaftis & Vlahogianni 2011), and hybrid methods (Jiang *et al.* 2014). A few statistical methods are used to analyze and predict traffic occurrence duration time. These are linear or nonparametric regression models (Garib *et al.* 1997).

Several data mining–machine learning methods are employed to predict traffic flow. These approaches are the classification trees model (CTM) (Kim *et al.* 2008), decision trees (DT), artificial neural networks (ANN) (Lee & Wei 2010), genetic algorithms (GA) (Valenti *et al.* 2010), and support/relevance vector machines (SVM/RVM). Many researchers have developed a hybrid method (Kim & Chang 2012) for prediction. Short-term traffic prediction (Jiang *et al.* 2014) may be used for several applications instead of no prediction or inaccurate prediction. Short-term prediction can be better applied on free-flow traffic in urban areas. This prediction technique reduces traffic congestion. The problem to be solved is whether traffic flow can be predicted ahead of time.

Intelligent transportation systems (ITS) are indispensable in proposing solutions to these types of problems. However, the high volume of vehicles involved in urban transportation creates the demand for the use of Big Data analytics to process and utilize the traffic system in an optimized way (Vlahogianni *et al.* 2014). Regression techniques are proposed to model vehicle arrivals based on real-time data (Lippi *et al.* 2013). In this paper, they introduced a new model for controlling the behavior of traffic systems. High-end software systems are required for real-time traffic planning, which is a challenge. The need to integrate the proposed form with other traffic simulation techniques has to be addressed. Intelligent Transport Systems provide techniques for traffic prediction (Lv *et al.* 2014), which requires precise traffic flow information. This is most significant in deploying intelligent transportation systems. Traffic data have been enlarging and increasing over the past decade. We are in the era of Big Data analytics for transportation management and control. To study the features of generic traffic flow, a stacked auto encoder model is used. This research utilized a traffic prediction model that focuses on spatial and temporal correlations. The prediction layer in the proposed system uses logistic regression. A sophisticated deep learning algorithm is needed to effectively route city traffic.

In their paper, Bowman and Miller (2016) used real-world big traffic data to examine the construction of traffic simulations. They used data to generate models for the arrival of vehicles, turning behavior, and traffic flow. They built a microscopic traffic simulation based on real-world data. The strengths and weaknesses of various simulation optimization techniques are addressed. The key motivation of this paper is to improve the efficiency, safety, and cost of road systems as this is a crucial social problem that must be solved. A traffic flow prediction algorithm was proposed with LWL (locally weighted learning), based on local models, and this uses local linear/nonlinear models to fit the nearest points and then uses their values to compute the values of the query points for prediction. This method uses the values of historical data. Accurate short-term traffic flow prediction was deployed within freeway networks. They proposed a traffic flow structure pattern. This technique was especially suitable for abnormal traffic flow states.

Accurate traffic prediction (Liu *et al.* 2016) has been proposed as a traffic estimation method, which makes use of road network correlation and sparse traffic sampling. This research was carried out in the city of Shanghai, China. The results proved that the proposed method reveals the hidden structure of traffic correlations. In resolving the destination prediction on location-based services, a novel model, T-DesP (Li *et al.* 2016), is proposed. An algorithm for short-term traffic flow forecasting is proposed (Lu *et al.* 2015). This algorithm uses a traffic correlation model and presents a coefficient optimization algorithm. To reduce traffic accidents and to save lives, a method for predicting future accidents in advance was required (Park *et al*. 2016). This would reduce accidents and save lives on roads. The proposed work used a Hadoop framework to process and analyze huge amounts of traffic data efficiently.

Genetic algorithms (GAs) have a role in various domains. They play a vital role in providing a system for traffic prediction and support the avoidance of traffic congestion. A genetic algorithm is necessary to determine the global minimum in the search area. This is a heuristic method. John Holland was the first to develop a mathematical form of GA (Holland 1975). GAs are capable of resolving problems using "the string" fitness to direct the search. This is the most important advantage of GAs when compared with other search methods. This does not require any definite knowledge regarding the search space. It works on population and this requires only a distinct measure of flow. This compares an individual to another individual. A model based on deep belief networks (DBNs) is proposed to predict traffic flow (Zhang & Huang 2018). This model employs a genetic algorithm to find the optimal hyper-parameters. An advanced time delay neural network (TDNN) model using a GA is proposed for short-term traffic flow prediction. This model proved that the proposed model is superior to well-known neural work models (Abdulhai *et al*. 2002). A multilayered structural optimization strategy based on a genetic algorithm is used for appropriate representation of traffic flow data with spatial and temporal characteristics (Vlahogianni *et al*. 2008). GACE (Lopez-Garcia *et al*. 2015) is a hybrid method that integrates a GA and cross-entropy (CE). The results proved that the proposed hybrid method is efficient in predicting short-term traffic congestion. For a very short traffic prediction for an interval of 5 minutes, a hybrid lane-based genetic algorithm has been proposed (Raza & Zhong 2017). To represent the actual travel patterns of a considerable amount of vehicles in a city, an approach based on a GA was developed. This finds an optimal origin destination (OD) matrix, providing an opportunity to plan and analyze the traffic scenario (Saini *et al*. 2015). A GA approach has been developed to locate an optimal OD matrix, viewing the actual travel patterns of a considerable number of vehicles within the city.

An adaptive genetic algorithm (Vandewater *et al*. 2015) is based on population size, which helps in determining mutation probability as well as crossover probability. These values are dependent on the fitness value, based on the population cover. The systems with fairly high fitness function values are found to perform better than those with less fitness value. When the population is in outer space, the probability value decreases, and it rises as the population approaches the local minima.

Feature representation (de Paula *et al*. 2016) is very important for creating any model based on machine learning. It indicates that any genetic programming technique is being used to change the feature space. Fitness function is very important because it helps in determining the feature space. The various functions are compared and a framework is proposed to automate the process.

The path optimization is targeted by the genetic algorithm (Lamini *et al*. 2018), which helps in determining a feasible path with less hindrance. A fitness function is proposed which takes into account various measures like energy, distance, and safety, which help in the convergence of the algorithm for better results. To address traffic congestion issues, a smart transportation system is proposed, which can handle traffic issues efficiently and prevents traffic congestion. The first section provides for the traffic identification and prediction system, and the latter section facilitates the avoidance scheme. The evaluation shows the efficiency of the proposed system in terms of energy and time.

2.5 Short-Term Traffic Prediction Model

Predicting short-term traffic flow is one of the challenging tasks in abnormal traffic situations, and this is key to utilizing collected traffic data efficiently, thereby predicting traffic flow in a given period of time (usually 5–20 minutes). In the 1970s, the ARIMA (autoregressive integrated moving average) model was used to predict short-term traffic flow in freeway networks (Ahmed & Cook 1979). Time-series is the major factor in almost any traffic flow prediction model. A local linear regression model was used in short-term traffic forecasting (Sun *et al*. 2003). In the same traffic flow forecasting, a Bayesian network approach was employed (Sun *et al*. 2006) to predict short-term traffic flow, and a support vector–based online learning weighted support vector regression approach were proposed (Jeong *et al*. 2013). Many researchers have focused on providing an efficient solution for traffic management and control. The focus was turned on machine learning techniques, which provided a path for academics and industries to focus their attention on smart intelligent transport management systems (SITMS).

A prediction methodology based on deep learning was proposed (Lv *et al*. 2014) for analyzing the system. A stacked auto encoder model was employed in a greedy layer-wise fashion. An approach for forecasting travel speed for multi-step-ahead based on 2-min travel speed data using fuzzy neural networks was proposed (Tang *et al*. 2017). The proposed mechanism was applied to the traffic data gathered from remote microwave sensors which were located on a southbound segment of a fourth ring road in Beijing City. The proposed approach results proved that this was an efficient mechanism and was better than the traditional models. A dynamic traffic simulator was designed (Abadi *et al*. 2014) to create flows in all links with available traffic information, demand, and historical traffic data obtainable from links set with sensors. The proposed scheme applies the simulator to alter the origin-to-destination matrices. To predict the traffic flow on each available link up to 30 min ahead, real-time and estimated traffic data was used. This proposed prediction algorithm was also based on an autoregressive model.

The traffic flow prediction algorithm has its own benefits and drawbacks. Few of the existing approaches can be applied on undisciplined traffic. Some prediction models of traffic flow have been developed recently which can be employed in abnormal conditions. The Online – Support Vector Regression model (Liu *et al*. 2007) was used in predicting traffic, especially during holidays. Some researchers have used neural networks to predict traffic during abnormal weather conditions. The drawback of the existing methods is that there is no analysis of the traffic structure between the current section and the upstream section. In this work, we propose an efficient short-term traffic prediction methodology. This was analyzed with a case study that considered one of the metropolitan cities of the Asian continent. This case study uses toll data in a freeway network. The toll data contains information about the entry and exit of vehicles in the freeway network. Using the collected traffic data, source and destination can be obtained. The traffic flow structure pattern can be extracted with the assistance of video cameras installed at the toll. With the collected information, we can reveal the relationships among the traffic flow on the current road section and the upstream stations. This information will support in predicting and avoiding traffic congestion, especially in abnormal traffic conditions.

2.6 Traffic Light Controller and Deviation System

The National Electrical Manufacturers Association (NEMA) has categorized controllers into two types: fixed controller and traffic response controller. Most of the proposed solutions and frameworks and several algorithmic schemas have used fixed cyclic time controllers. In their paper, Chiu and Chand (1993) proposed an approach that involves altering the fixed type controller approach. These controllers were programmed to function at preset timings for each series. This solution was used for various types of traffic scenarios and especially for undisciplined traffic. Several research algorithms had focused on avoiding the fixed cyclic controller system, but ITS still needs an efficient approach to reduce traffic problems. Addressing a single issue may not be an efficient solution; several parameters have to be considered to avoid traffic congestion in advance. Vehicle speed and length are considered the two most important factors in traffic management systems.

VANET is a technology that considers vehicles as a node in a network and creates a mobile network for data exchange and communication, where each vehicle will participate in exchanging information related to traffic conditions. VANETs provide better techniques to collect and deliver real-time traffic related information in a cost effective manner (Hartenstein & Laberteaux 2009). V2V and V2R communications in VANETs helps to gather traffic updates from vehicles and road side units. This gathered traffic data helps in providing a freeway traffic flow and can be used for path planning and vehicle localization (Hunter *et al.* 2009). A simple V2V and V2R communication exchange is shown in Figure. 2.3. To collect real-time traffic related information, most of the techniques rely on mobile and loop detectors. Since cellular phones are not equipped for traffic information exchange,

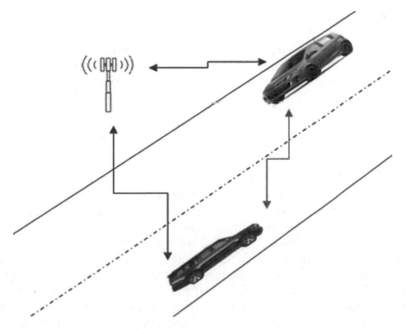

FIGURE 2.3
V2V and V2R communication.

these services are expensive, and congestion results in a large quantity of traffic data. The expenses involved in implementing loop detector systems are very high (Wang *et al.* 2014). An incompetent system creates delays in communication and a resulting degradation of safety. Timing and security issues in ITS with VANETs are addressed (Zheng *et al.* 2017).

Floating car data is used to provide a feasible automated incident detection system (Houbraken *et al.* 2017). The automated systems depend on the traffic monitoring sensors that are installed in the roads. Some approaches have been proposed to track vehicles based on real-time data and video processing units (Cai *et al.* 2010). Feature-based vehicle flow detection and measurement parameters are addressed to identify the vehicle flow (Huang *et al.* 2012). A novel multiple inductive loop sensor system was proposed to detect vehicles in mixed and lane-less traffic (Ali *et al.* 2011). The proposed loop sensor detects vehicles based on their size and occupancy. This system separates the vehicle types and determines the quantity of vehicles in a mixed traffic stream. A method for classifying the vehicles based on Fourier transform (Lamas-Seco *et al.* 2015) with a single loop is proposed to improve the traffic management system. Categorization (Ki & Baik 2006) and evaluation (De Lima *et al.* 2010) based on a single-loop system are used widely. (Wang, S *et al.* 2018) proposed a prediction model based on a nonparametric regression approach.

The problem of achieving accuracy using only one loop is yet to be resolved. The transportation infrastructure can be integrated with various advanced sensor technologies to achieve a feasible smart and intelligent transportation system. The benefits of employing multiple sensors on different elements in a traffic management system are discussed (Guerrero-Ibáñez *et al.* 2018). Some protocols are addressed to work with wireless sensor networks (Tong & Tang 2010). In Taghvaeeyan and Rajamani (2013), a classification approach is proposed which is based on magnetic length. The vehicles are categorized into four groups, and this overcomes the disadvantage of existing techniques. The length of the vehicle can also be measured using the magnetic length. Group I and II vehicles are compared within the same group by means of the Group III and Group IV vehicles, since there is dissimilarity in their length. The overall traffic weight was calculated based on the precedence in Samadi *et al.* (2012), and the sum of the sensors was computed. Thus, we propose computing the overall traffic weight depending on its comparative weight, speed, and length to enhance the effectiveness of the system.

2.7 IoT-Based Intelligent Transportation Systems

In 2010, the European Union defined intelligent transportation systems (ITS) as systems "in which information and communication technologies are applied in the field of road transport, including infrastructure, vehicles and users, and in traffic management and mobility management, as well as for interfaces with other modes of transport".

Smart transportation includes the use of several technologies, from basic management systems such as car navigation, traffic signal control systems, container management systems, automatic number plate recognition, or speed cameras to monitor applications, such as security CCTV systems, and more advanced applications that integrate live data and feedback from a number of other sources. ITS technologies allow users to make better use of the transportation network and also pave the way for the development of smarter infrastructure to meet future demands. The evolution of intelligent transportation systems is providing a growing number of technology solutions for transportation managers as they seek to operate and maintain the systems more efficiently and improve performance.

According to the Intelligent Transportation Society of America, ITS technology makes it possible to:

- Use a navigation system to find the best route based on real-time conditions.
- Alert drivers of potentially hazardous situations in time to avoid crashes.
- Be guided to an empty parking space by a smart sign.
- Ride a bus that turns traffic lights green on approach.
- Detect and respond promptly to traffic incidents.
- Reroute traffic in response to road conditions or weather emergencies.
- Give travelers real-time traffic and weather reports.
- Allow drivers to manage their fuel consumption.
- Adjust speed limits and signal timing based on real-world conditions.
- Improve freight tracking, inspection, safety and efficiency.
- Make public transportation more convenient and reliable.
- Monitor the structural integrity of bridges and other infrastructure.

An example of the benefits of the implementation of smart transportation technologies can be found in Austria, where the country's Autobahn and Highway Financial Stock Corporation (ASFiNAG) turned to Cisco's Connected Roadways solutions to bring the Internet of Things (IoT) to its roadside sensors. The result is a highway designed to monitor itself, send information to drivers, and predict traffic to ensure lanes stay clear of congestion.

By all accounts, the Internet of Things and Big Data represents a huge opportunity for cost savings and new revenue generation across a broad range of industries. Researchers provided a primer on IoT and described how IoT impacts the manufacturing industry in the first two briefs in the IoT series. This brief will highlight several examples of how IoT is being used to create smarter cities. In its most basic definition, the Internet of Things describes a system whereby items in the physical world, and sensors within or attached to these items, are connected to the Internet via wireless and wired network connections. The Internet of Things will connect inanimate objects as well as living things – everything from industrial equipment to everyday objects that range from medical devices to automobiles to utility meters.

Aceves and Paddack (2002) deal with developing an analysis environment for systems to analyze and optimize the Intelligent Transport System (ITS). This uses the phenomenon of the co-simulation, which helps in modeling systems with high flexibility. The concept of virtual ITS is implemented by selecting various components which run on different platforms. These components are simulated by using pre-existing packages, such that all of the packages operate with same time stamp or in multiples of the smallest time stamp. Thus the proposed system is cost effective by avoiding the need for calculation in real time. The integrated system analysis environment developed helps ITS with the seamless integration of various models, thereby assembling the existing structure that functions far better than the existing models. Thus the process of the system integration is streamlined and the ITS setup is designed to be implemented throughout the country without any obstacles. The proposed application of the co-simulation concept for ITS can be extended to incorporate timing, thus making it a time-based simulation.

An efficient traffic light system is proposed by Shandiz *et al.* (2009), which uses a genetic algorithm for evaluating the stochastic data, thereby arriving at an optimized transport system. The data is processed, each traffic light is coded, and then the cumulative information for each route is calculated to find the optimum state. The simulation is done based on the route length and average speed of the vehicles. The simulation helps to find the optimum state in which the maximum number of vehicles can move with the proposed traffic lights. The simultaneous analysis of more objects using a statistical measure is given through multivariate analysis by Hair, William, Barry, and Rolphe (2010). By this technique, simultaneous analysis occurs on more than two variables. Various multivariate analysis techniques have been proposed which could be applied as needed.

Petracca *et al.* (2013) propose a prototype of vehicle which is capable of interacting with other roadside vehicles and also with an internal electronic device. The model also specifies the various components adopted in the proposed on-board unit. This also provides various applications that could use this technique for efficient operations. The proposed work gives an overview of the various requirements for designing an efficient ITS system. Based on a real-world scenario, simulations are done using MATLAB to determine the accuracy of the proposed system. The observations show that the proposed environment helps in identifying vehicle position in different environments. The algorithm is analyzed in terms of running time and also based on the accuracy of the results. In de la Garza *et al.* (2013), a new system is proposed that integrates Internet of Things with the proposed intelligent transportation system so as to provide better transportation. In Bojan *et al.* (2014), the sensors are used to monitor the environment, which is then used by the monitoring system to inform drivers regarding the positioning of the device and details pertaining to it. Thus the data is displayed as the current bus route for the passengers. This system determines the number of tickets obtained as it decides the efficiency of the proposed technique. Table 2.3 shows some IoT-based ITSs.

TABLE 2.3

Survey on IoT-Based Intelligent Traffic System

Author	Publication Year	Proposed Technique	Traffic Safety	Energy Efficient	Merits
Grob	2009	Pollution-free Transportation	No	Yes	Handles traffic in an efficient manner
Costa & Seixas	2014	Pollution-avoidance transportation	Yes	Yes	Reduction in emission of CO_2 by using electric vehicles
Mehar *et al.*	2014	Green transportation	No	Yes	Traffic handling with sustainability is prioritized
Iturrate *et al.*	2015	Safe and sustainable transportation	Yes	Yes	Traffic congestion is handled efficiently
Harilakshmi & Rani	2016	Green transportation	Yes	No	Proposes a pollution-free technique which helps in vehicular movement
Abdalla & Abaker	2016	Collision-free transportation	Yes	No	Determination of braking response time and steering response time
Petrov *et al.*	2017	Collision-free transportation	Yes	Yes	Safe system design with collision warning
Agarwal *et al.*	2018	Congestion avoidance transportation	Yes	Yes	Time of arrival (TOA)–based localization, using automatic braking for collision avoidance

Source: World Economic Forum.

2.8 Summary

Various techniques have been implemented (e.g., ANN, SVM, ARIMA), but the outcomes are not satisfactory. Existing techniques have not paid enough attention to the quality of the data under analysis. ANN is not reliable when the training data is not explanatory of the real pattern and the training data proportions are not sufficient. The SVM model suffers from dimensions during data analysis and requires a long time. ARIMA is the most common and traditional model, featuring a simple algorithm based on a linear analysis which is not sufficient to predict the stochastic nature of traffic series data. There has been no investigation that tries to link the count of traffic data with information from other sources, such as the season, the weather, the impact of events (traffic accident, planned or unplanned road construction), the time of day, and the day of the week. Therefore, a smart framework is needed for the domain of transportation which performs traffic prediction with a fuel consumption model and analyzes traffic flow congestion using a genetic and regression model. Based on a multi-agent system, it would control traffic lights and deviate the traffic route.

A traffic flow prediction system using a neural network has been proposed (Jiber *et al.* 2018). The proposed framework employs deep learning architecture to predict road traffic flow. This has the ability to reconstruct lost data with the predicted values, but there are certain limitations. The proposed method loses its ability to predict the traffic in unexpected conditions and on abnormal days. Yao *et al.* (2017) proposed a method to predict short-term traffic speed using a support vector machine model. The prediction accuracy of this method is lessened when the traffic speed is higher than 35 km/h, and thereby the performance of the technique is reduced.

A traffic flow prediction method using a Kalman filtering technique has been proposed (Kumar *et al.* 2017) which uses real-time data as well as historical data. The limitations of this method are that it uses only 2 days' worth of historical data; moreover, there is no way to handle the missing values. The performance of the system is good only with datasets without noisy data.

A traffic flow forecasting method was proposed (Omkar *et al.* 2017) to forecast traffic flow using a time series decomposition model. The proposed work requires a smaller amount of data and can handle both real-time and historical data. It fails to address external factors such as accidents and weather, however. The performance of the system will be degraded when there are missing data. Zhang *et al.* (2016) proposed a real-time traffic flow prediction method using augmented reality. The proposed technique has been shown to have improved accuracy. The drawback with this method is that the data used to forecast is made synthetically, and thus it does not consider chaotic situations.

Khandelwal *et al.* (2015) recommended that neither ANN nor ARIMA is generally appropriate for time series of all types. Every real-world time series holds both nonlinear and linear correlation structures among the annotations. Khandelwal *et al.* (2015) specified a novel hybrid approach which utilized DWT to change the time series in the nonlinear and linear components. Based on this technique, the proposed technique will have the benefit of changing time-series information into linear time series information. Further, it will be used in the final forecasting model ARIMA to predict the result.

A Big Data–based traffic flow prediction method has been proposed (Lv *et al.* 2014) using a deep learning approach. This examines historical and real-time data to be used as input in a greedy approach which provides an incredible performance. However, it requires huge amounts of time to process and fetch the results, and this is also expensive. The data used are produced synthetically in this approach.

The drawback with the existing work is that most of the methods fail to deal with abnormal traffic situations. These methods have addressed only certain attributes; moreover, they cannot be applied to undisciplined traffic and some cannot be used for freeway traffic. Thereby the performance of the existing works is diminished and is not capable of dealing with traffic in abnormal circumstances. Existing designs do not deal with traffic prediction, or with intelligent traffic light control systems. The drawback of the existing methods is that there is no analysis of the traffic structure between the current section and upstream section.

These limitations with the existing methods have to be overcome. Most researchers have used neural networks, support vector machines, and genetic algorithms to predict traffic during abnormal conditions. Most of the methods available in the literature provide traffic prediction methodologies, and few provide congestion control algorithms.

In our research work, we have provided solutions in terms of procedures, techniques, and algorithms to fill the gap between the current issues and the existing approaches. We have focused on both regular traffic flow and short-term traffic flow. We have also considered intelligent traffic light controlling and parking systems. Moreover, the proposed framework also integrates time and fuel consumption models. Our proposed framework can also act as an intelligent traffic light control and deviation system and also has the capability to assist emergency vehicles to reach hospitals in a shorter time. The proposed framework is suitable for the traffic system in India.

To address these traffic congestion issues, a smart transportation system is proposed which can handle traffic issues efficiently and avoids traffic congestion. The evaluation shows the efficiency of the proposed system in terms of energy and time. The accuracy of the prediction method is most important in abnormal traffic states and especially during peak hours. The prediction of the traffic flow structure pattern will enhance the accuracy of the prediction system. This system is better able to handle sudden increases in traffic flow and can support determining the maximum traffic flow in the given duration.

3

Smart Traffic Prediction and Congestion Avoidance System (S-TPCA) Using Genetic Predictive Models for Urban Transportation

3.1 Introduction

Road traffic congestion is a persistent problem worldwide. With the huge growth in the population, the number of vehicles is increasing at a faster rate. This results in traffic congestion, which is a major issue in urban transportation. This is an extreme problem faced in almost all major cities in India. In this chapter, the Indian traffic system is considered. The proposals discussed are appropriate to Indian cities, but can also be employed in cities in other nations. Since the Indian traffic system is chaotic and non-lane based, this is different from Western traffic. The problem is felt in all major cities, since there has been a great increase in the population and the number of vehicles; space, cost, and infrastructure is a major problem, which leads to heavy traffic congestion. In many nations, an intelligent transport system (ITS) helps avoid congestion and makes the traffic system efficient. These kinds of technologies cannot be used in India, however. The Indian traffic system scenario is different from other countries. Therefore, intelligent traffic systems should be altered so as to be suitable for the characteristics of Indian roads. Due to the development of building infrastructure, metro rail systems, and road enlargement, traffic congestion is becoming a huge problem in all metropolitan cities. Some Indian cities have seen surprising growth in the IT sector and also abrupt growth in their population. Bangalore, Delhi-NCR, Hyderabad, and Pune are some of the cities where traffic congestion issues are increasing every day. Providing a solution to resolve traffic issues needs infrastructure growth also. Space and cost are the primary constraints in improving traffic scenarios.

3.2 Smart Traffic Prediction

Nowadays, smart city services are becoming more widespread than ever before as cities are growing and becoming increasingly crowded as a result of urbanization and world population growth. The term "smart city" refers to the use of information and communication technologies to sense, analyze, and integrate key information from core systems in operating cities. At the same time, smart city services can make intelligent responses to different kinds of needs in terms of daily livelihood, environmental protection, and public safety, as well as the city's facilities and industrial and commercial activities.

DOI: 10.1201/9781003217367-3

Among the various notable goals of smart cities, the construction of smart transportation systems and smart urban management systems are two of the key aims, which could significantly influence the lives of residents in future cities. Advanced traffic management systems (ATMSs) and intelligent transportation systems (ITSs) integrate information, communication, and other technologies and apply them in the field of transportation to build an integrated system of people, roads, and vehicles. These systems constitute a large, fully functioning, real-time, accurate, and efficient transportation management framework.

In ATMSs and ITSs, it is a fundamental challenge to predict upcoming possible states of traffic with high precision, because this information helps to prevent unfortunate events like traffic jams or other anomalies on roads. The chapter often refers to traffic as a flow, because it has similar properties to fluids. Thus, when we speak about traffic flow prediction, we wish to predict the upcoming state of the traffic flow based on historic and real-time data.

3.3 Congestion Avoidance System

Many cities have long been notorious for their serious traffic congestion; Beijing, for example, China's capital, has been one of the world's most congested cities for many years. The traffic situation especially deteriorates during rush hours. According to the Global Commuter Pain Survey, released by IBM in 2011, 69 percent of those surveyed indicated that traffic has negatively affected their health in some way. Therefore congestion avoidance is important for cities around the world.

To deal with this problem, this chapter proposes a smart traffic prediction and congestion avoidance system (S-TPCA) which helps to better identify traffic scenarios, which in turn helps to predict and avoid congestion. The proposed work uses Poisson distribution for the prediction of vehicle arrivals from recurring size (the volume of vehicles occur again and thereby it checks for the fitness function for further process). This framework comprises traffic identification, prediction, and congestion avoidance phases. The system checks for the fitness function to determine traffic intensity and further uses predictive analytics to determine future traffic levels. This system also integrates a fuel consumption model to save time and energy.

3.4 Preliminaries

The use of probability and statistics applications is increasing at a greater rate in providing solutions to solve engineering problems. Intelligent transportation systems represent an interdisciplinary area that uses different mathematical models and data analytics to predict and prevent traffic congestion. Most of the probability techniques are useful in vehicular traffic. Poisson distribution is an appropriate model which can be applied for predicting the arrival of vehicles in traffic systems. Poisson distribution is a mathematical relationship used for such things as testing the randomness of a specified set of data, fitting empirical data to a theoretical curve, and predicting certain phenomena on the basis of basic data. Traffic engineers can apply this distribution technique to analyze the arrival rates of a vehicle at a given point in time. We use Poisson distribution for prediction of arrivals of recurring size.

Poisson distribution can be applied under the conditions of "free flow", in which is possible to calculate the probability of 0, 1, 2, 3, ..., k vehicles arriving per time interval of t seconds, provided the recurring size, R, is known:

t = time interval (seconds)

R = recurring volume

n = number of intervals

$$n = \frac{3600}{t}(per\ hour)$$

m = average amount of vehicles per interval

$$m = \frac{R}{\frac{3600}{t}} = \frac{Rt}{3600} \tag{3.1}$$

Then the probability, $P(v)$, that v vehicles will arrive at some point in any interval is:

$$P(v) = \frac{m^v e^{-m}}{v!} = \frac{1}{v!}\left(\frac{Rt}{3600}\right)^{ve^{-\frac{vt}{3600}}} \tag{3.2}$$

The hourly frequency, F_v, of intervals including v vehicles is:

$$F_v = nP(v) = \left(\frac{3600}{t}\right)\frac{1}{v!}\left(\frac{Rt}{3600}\right)^{ve^{-\frac{vt}{3600}}} \tag{3.3}$$

If the considered period is different from an hour, the 3600 can be substituted by the proper time period in seconds.

3.5 TPCA System

Transportation systems are proposed to improve transportation services such as secure and safe travel, travel reliability, road safety, informed travel choices, transport productivity, environmental protection, and traffic resilience. We propose to predict the traffic congestion based on the arrival time of vehicles; this will help to reduce traffic congestion before it occurs. This may not solve the problem completely, but it can be an efficient way to improve the Indian traffic system. Along with prediction, other benefits that can be achieved are the rerouting of vehicles, savings in fuel consumption, and the protection of the environment. Speed advice for drivers before reaching the signal will allow them to drive their vehicle based on the available time interval. This provides a better chance of avoiding pollution, as the waiting time in the traffic will be reduced. Travelers and drivers can benefit from these kinds of traffic control systems.

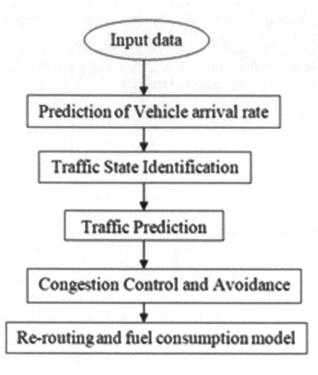

FIGURE 3.1
S-TPCA Framework.

This will lead to an improvement in urban traffic conditions in the city, where predictions can be made of vehicles' arrival. We evaluated the prediction technique in low recurring volume and high recurring volume. We collected information on the arrival of the vehicles manually during low and moderate volumes of traffic, and the same was evaluated. Testing the suitability of the information with a Poisson distribution was performed with x^2 test for its acceptance or rejection. A huge volume of data can be collected and maintained in a cloud-based environment. The proposed framework flow is shown in Figure 3.1.

3.5.1 Gathering Traffic Data

The traffic system in various places follows a structure as it deals with the lives of human beings. The traffic data for processing is obtained through various sensors and by constant monitoring, which enables the S-TPCA to apply parameters for further processing. The information from the sensor is then fed into the traffic system, which helps to properly address the traffic conditions. The sensors provide information about the arrival time of the vehicles and the frequency at which they arrive as well as the count of the vehicles. These are the primary parameters based on which the process of traffic prediction and congestion avoidance works.

The traffic flow is dynamic in any area and so determining the traffic state is based on the traffic parameters. So the estimation is done based on the relationship between the parameters and also the traffic state as follows:

$$Q = SP(w, \vartheta, \rho) \tag{3.4}$$

where SP defines the relationship that holds between the traffic flow and traffic parameters. Here the traffic parameters are (w, ϑ, ρ). Traffic will be mostly dynamic in an area. This means a time-series is created which alters with time t.

$$T_t = R\left(T_{e-1}, T_{e-2}, \dots\right) \tag{3.5}$$

Here T_t describes flow parameter T at time t with function R to determine the series of data flow. Further, the data is judged based on the historical data, and then the relation between the two can be depicted as

$$T_{w,t} = R\left(T_{w-1,t}, T_{w-2,t}, \dots\right) \tag{3.6}$$

where $T_{w,t}$ denotes traffic flow parameters recorded on a particular day of the week at time t. "R" defines the relationship between the data signifying the day of the week as a holiday or workday with respect to time.

Real-time data from a particular location is gathered using sensors and the data is continuously stored and updated in the distributed system. So when a vehicle moves, its movement pattern is recorded in SP (the relationship parameter, expressed in equation 3.4) with the traffic parameters and it changes with time T_t. The gathered real-time data is then processed with the proposed traffic prediction algorithm and, based on the historical traffic data from the particular location, the decision algorithm helps to avoid congestion and allow easy movement of vehicles.

There are hundreds of parameters on which the traffic system depends. The major parameters which contribute to traffic management include the velocity of the vehicle, the arrival time of the vehicle, the average number of vehicles, the travel time of the vehicle, vehicle occupancy, the length of the vehicle etc. There are various parameters in determining the traffic flow in a particular region. The factors include vehicle velocity, arrival time, average distance, average speed, average length, composition speed, composition length, kamikaze alarm, etc. Of these parameters, the following parameters play a major role in the proposed algorithm. This is illustrated in Table 3.1.

3.5.2 Identification of Traffic State

The traffic scenario necessitates the calculation of the membership function and determining traffic congestion and the method of avoidance by proposing a new technique TPCA system. This technique uses the arrival time of the vehicle and also calculates the function using Poisson distribution. Algorithm 3.1 shows the proposed TPCA algorithm.

TABLE 3.1

List of Parameters

Parameter	Notation
Velocity	v
Average number of vehicles	m
Total number of vehicles	T_p
Arrival time	A_t
Arrival interval	A_i
Maximum speed of the vehicle	Speed
Travel time of the vehicle	t
Length of the vehicle	L

3.5.2.1 Min–Max Normalization

Min–max normalization is a normalization strategy which linearly transforms x to

$$y = (x - min)/(max - min)$$

where min and max are the minimum and maximum values in X, where X is the set of observed values of x. It can be easily seen that when $x = min$, then $y = 0$, and when $x = max$, then $y = 1$. This means that the minimum value in X is mapped to 0 and the maximum value in X is mapped to 1. So, the entire range of values of X from min to max is mapped to the range from 0 to 1.

Algorithm 3.1: TPCA Algorithm with Modified FCM Algorithm

Step 1: Value initialization: total population T_p, arriving intervals A_i, arrival time A_t, genetic criteria G_c

Step 2: Redefined TPCA clustering algorithm:
    Arbitrarily select k vehicles as the initial centers
    Until no change, do

Step 3: Assign the vehicle to the cluster with the similar parameters. Improve the quality of the centers selected

Step 4: For each pair of selection B and other vehicles V
    Calculate the cost $TC_{BV} = \sum_j C_{jBV}$
    Derive membership function μ_{ij}

    Subject to $\sum_{i=0}^{N} \mu_{ij} = 1$, $0 \leq \mu_{ij} \leq 1$

    Where $\mu_{ij} = 1/n \sum_{i=0} (Dg_{ij}/Dg_{kj})^{2/(s-1)}$, if $Dg_{ij} \geq 0$

    1 if $Dg_{ij} = 0$, $i = j$
    0 if $Dg_{ij} = 0$, $i \neq j$

Step 5: Calculate the fitness value of each object fn_i

Step 6: Initial genetic criteria $G_{c=0}$

Step 7: Perform genetic functions like mutation of the original arrival time of the vehicles

Step 8: Compute mutation results G_cM
i. Calculate new membership function μ'
ii. Calculate new fitness value f'

Step 9: Fitness comparison: if $f' > f$, replace the old values with the new objects
Else replace the old value with probability factor $p = \exp(f' = f) q$ where q is the constant

Step 10: Arrive at the CDF with respect to time and fuel consumption

The graph in Figure 3.2 depicts the effect on the application of genetic mutation, which results in making an effort to identify the traffic state of the location based on the arrival time and judge the cumulative density function accordingly.

Further, this data is used to compare the performance of the proposed technique with the existing ones to ensure the sustainability and scalability of the new technique. Here the algorithm specifies the threshold value f, which is between 0 and 1.0 and specifies the normal motion of vehicles in the road, whereas the values up to 0.40 specify moderate traffic conditions on the road. Values higher than 0.40 are a warning sign indicating heavy traffic if the threshold moves beyond 0.40.

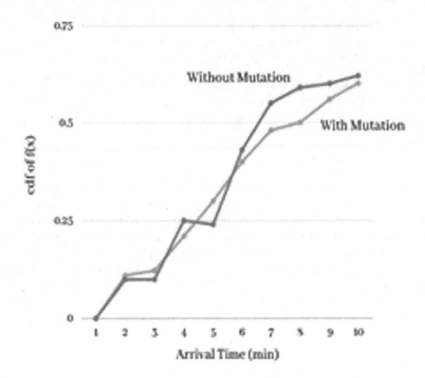

FIGURE 3.2
Depiction of applying mutation on the vehicle movement.

3.5.3 Traffic Prediction and Congestion Avoidance

Traffic can be reduced by diverting vehicles via another road. This will improve traffic conditions in the city, where predictions can be made of vehicle arrival. We evaluate the prediction technique in conditions of high recurring volume. A huge volume of data can be collected and maintained in a cloud-based environment.

```
Algorithm 3.2: Prediction and Avoidance
(1) Detect trajectory
Step 1: Start, finish <- 0
Step 2: D_aF <- Dataframe
Step 3: For i in DataFrameindex do
Step 4: If DataFrame[K].speed = 0 then
        Finish <- k
Step 5: While D_aF[k].speed = 0 do
        i <- i + 1
Finish new <- i
Step 6: If D_aF[finish new].time- D_aF[finish].time > threshold then
Index[trips] <- range(start,Finish)
        Start <- Finish new + 1
Step 7: While D_aF[start].speed = 0 do
        Start <- start + 1
        End < -k

(2) Traffic prediction and control
Initialize j⁰ = {θ}, s_t(θ) = 0 for all tєτ, H⁰ = 0
        Step 1: For each traffic prediction (time t) does
```

```
Step 2: Calculate Dⁱ ∈ jⁱ such that θⁱ ∈ Dⁱ
Step 3: Generate results for predictors t(xⁱ) for all t
Step 4: Final prediction selection yⁱ = t*(xⁱ)
Step 5: Correct traffic pattern yⁱ is estimated
Step 6: Update the mean sample sₜ(Dⁱ) for all t
Step 7: Hⁱ_c = Hⁱ_c + 1
Step 8: If Hⁱ_c > x2ᵖˡ then
Step 9: Dⁱ is further categorized
Step 10: End if
Step 11: End for
```

The major task of (1) is to identify the vehicle in a group of other vehicles using working units, namely trajectories. This enables the vehicle to slow down or stop when it reaches a certain threshold value, but they are all computed into one component. Once the trajectories are fixed, the prediction algorithm helps in predicting and controlling the traffic.

(2) Gives the prediction of the traffic in subspace D^i that belongs to the partition j^i. The algorithm activates the predictors and predictions are made as $t(x^i)$ for all t. The predictor with the highest value is selected. Thus a Big Data technique is used to predict traffic using the trajectories of the various vehicles. Hence, based on the traffic prediction, the expected congestion can be avoided by rerouting the vehicles via the location which has the minimum traffic.

3.5.4 Rerouting and Fuel Consumption Model

Traffic management and driving patterns play a major role in the design of eco-friendly fuel consumption models. Fuel consumption can be roughly estimated on the basis of the effective traffic structure as well as driving behavior. Freight is a major cause of air pollution and so must be taken into consideration for effective model design.

The vehicle's emission calculation is based on the speed at which the vehicle moves and also the acceleration that is applied to the vehicle, which is given as

$$X = a + 0.014v \tag{3.7}$$

where v is in km/hr and a is in m/s²

Table 3.2 shows the design of the fuel consumption model in various schemes. The proposed scheme is both simulation-based and analytical. It is similar to the A_m scheme, yet the advanced scheme allows for simulations as well as applying a mathematical concept to determine fuel consumption. Thus the proposed model is more energy efficient than existing systems. The proposed TPCA model involves minimization of the traffic by rerouting

TABLE 3.2

Comparison of Fuel Consumption Model with Various Techniques

Technique	Fuel Consumption Model	
	Simulation Based	Analytical
Proposed TPCA	Yes	Yes
A_m	Yes	Yes
AQ	No	Yes
$A^\varnothing$	Yes	No

it through areas with lower levels of traffic. Heavier vehicles move on the city's highways, while other vehicles are diverted via routes with minimal traffic.

3.6 Experiment Results and Discussion

This work proposed an S-TPCA system for a metropolitan city in India. The Indian traffic system is in need of smart intelligent traffic management and congestion avoidance system across various urban areas to control the traffic scenarios. Road traffic congestion is a major issue that affects air quality for many people. Road traffic congestion is also the main cause of many traffic accidents.

A survey of road traffic accident deaths is presented in Figure 3.3. Most urban areas in India are affected a lot by traffic issues as there has been a huge increase in the number of vehicles. When there are a large number of vehicles, speed and time are reduced and environmental pollution occurs. The various impacts of traffic congestion are illustrated in Figure 3.4. Table 3.3 shows the average speed of vehicles in traffic in India's most congested metropolitan cities. The overall average speed is 22.7 km/hr.

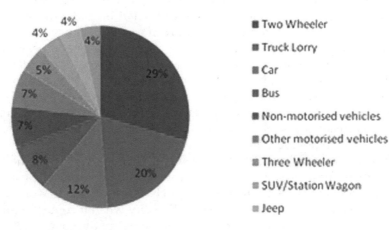

Percenatge of road accident deaths

- Two Wheeler
- Truck Lorry
- Car
- Bus
- Non-motorised vehicles
- Other motorised vehicles
- Three Wheeler
- SUV/Station Wagon
- Jeep

FIGURE 3.3
Road accident deaths by mode of transport.

TABLE 3.3

Average Speed of Vehicles in the Indian Traffic System

S. No.	Average Speed (09:00 AM to 12:00 PM) km/hr	Place
	27.1	Hyderabad
	26.5	Delhi-NCR
	21.9	Pune
	21.6	Mumbai
	20.4	Bangalore
	20.2	Kolkata
	19.6	Chennai

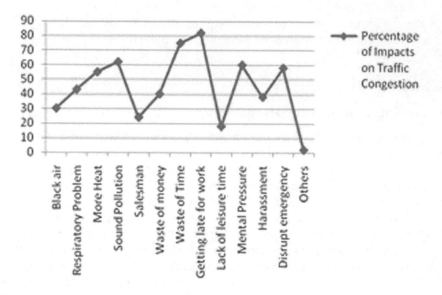

FIGURE 3.4
Impacts of traffic congestion.

Every big city suffers from the same predicament. Be it New York, London, or Chennai, traffic jams can leave commuters on the verge of mental breakdown. In summer, it is unbearable to mutely watch the red light turn green as the mercury rises steadily. The signals are placed randomly so locating them is a challenge – one appears on the right at an intersection, another is situated above your head elsewhere. If that doesn't confuse you, then the timing of the red lights will. Normally automatic, these turn manual with a traffic policeman trying to manage the flow during peak hours. There have been various solutions and suggestions put forth, but what seems to be a novel solution is "going smart".

New Delhi has already adopted a "smart" system whereby signals will soon be automatic. Recently, a Chennai-based NGO has developed a similar system. It will be intelligent enough to automatically adjust timings depending upon the volume of vehicles. When the time for traffic horror stories comes around, one can almost hear the collective sighs in Mumbai and Bangalore. Delhi, unfortunately, has some of the worst traffic in the country. Chennai, as it turns out, is the worst Indian city when it comes to traffic. In this work, we simulate our proposed smart traffic system in one of the congested traffic routes in Chennai. Chennai is the capital city of Tamil Nadu. According to the 2011 Indian census, it is the sixth largest city and fourth most populous urban agglomeration in India.

This work used a traffic flow dataset for traffic flow prediction and congestion avoidance. This dataset contains details of the traffic flow between Kumbakonam, Thanjavur, Trichy, and Madurai. It has 16 attributes, namely,

(1) Current_Location

(2) Destination

(3) Route

(4) Distance

(5) Average_Speed

(6) Time_to_Reach_Destination

(7) Date_&_Time

(8) Two_Wheeler

(9) Truck_Lorry

(10) Car

(11) Bus

(12) Non_Motorised_Vehicles

(13) Other_Motorised_Vehicles

(14) Three_Wheeler

(15) SUVOrStation_Wagon

(16) Jeep

SAMPLE DATASET

Current_Location, Destination, Route, Distance, Average_Speed, Time_to_ Reach_Destination, Date_&_Time, Two_Wheeler, Truck_Lorry, Car, Bus, Non_Motorised_Vehicles, Other_Motorised_Vehicles, Three_Wheeler, SUVOrStation_Wagon, Jeep

Kumbakonam, Madurai, Kumbakonam-Thiruvaiyaru-Thanjavur-Vallam-Trichy-Puthukkottai-Madurai, 280, 22.7, 12.3, 14-02-2020 09:45 PM, 12, 26, 68, 52, 53, 10, 90, 59, 25

Thanjavur, Trichy, Thanjavur-Vallam-Trichy, 120, 22.7, 5.3, 14-02-2020 09:50 PM, 52, 46, 24, 73, 96, 74, 31, 94, 99

Thanjavur, Madurai, Thanjavur-Vallam-Trichy-Puthukkottai-Madurai, 200, 22.7, 8.8, 15-02-2020 06:10 PM, 81, 94, 98, 74, 116, 91, 93, 84, 71

Madurai, Trichy, Madurai-Puthukkottai-Trichy, 120, 22.7, 5.3, 15-02-2020 08:10 AM, 88, 70, 80, 117, 114, 107, 72, 81, 89

Trichy, Kumbakonam, Trichy-Vallam-Thanjavur-Thiruvaiyaru-Kumbakonam, 200, 22.7, 8.8, 15-02-2020 08:00 AM, 78, 84, 80, 71, 80, 108, 119, 99, 108

Trichy, Kumbakonam, Trichy-Lalgudi-Thanjavur-Thirukkarugavur-Kumbakonam, 200, 22.7, 8.8, 14-02-2020 09:55 PM, 45, 22, 49, 29, 28, 41, 44, 28, 60

Kumbakonam, Madurai, Kumbakonam-Ayyampettai-Thanjavur-Kallanai-Trichy-Dindigul-Madurai, 280, 22.7, 12.3, 14-02-2020 09:45 PM, 18, 69, 40, 30, 41, 50, 50, 27, 99

Thanjavur, Trichy, Thanjavur-Kallanai-Trichy, 120, 22.7, 5.3, 14-02-2020 09:50 PM, 10, 24, 82, 67, 41, 94, 96, 15, 59

Kumbakonam, Trichy, Kumbakonam-Thiruvaiyaru-Thanjavur-Vallam-Trichy, 200, 22.7, 8.8, 15-02-2020 05:15 PM, 93, 82, 109, 113, 73, 119, 95, 113, 76

Madurai, Kumbakonam, Madurai-Puthukkottai-Trichy-Vallam-Thanjavur-Thiruvaiyaru-Kumbakonam, 280, 22.7, 12.3, 15-02-2020 05:35 PM, 87, 97, 113, 108, 78, 107, 83, 112, 118

Kumbakonam, Madurai, Kumbakonam-Thiruvaiyaru-Thanjavur-Vallam-Trichy-Puthukkottai-Madurai, 280, 22.7, 12.3, 15-02-2020 05:45 PM, 12, 26, 68, 52, 43, 20, 90, 69, 25

Thanjavur, Trichy, Thanjavur-Vallam-Trichy, 120, 22.7, 5.3, 15-02-2020 07:30 PM, 52, 46, 28, 73, 96, 74, 31, 94, 92

Thanjavur, Madurai, Thanjavur-Vallam-Trichy-Puthukkottai-Madurai, 210, 22.7, 8.8, 15-02-2020 07:45 PM, 81, 94, 98, 74, 116, 91, 93, 74, 65

Madurai, Trichy, Madurai-Puthukkottai-Trichy, 120, 22.7, 5.3, 15-02-2020 08:00 PM, 88, 70, 80, 117, 114, 108, 72, 80, 78

Trichy, Kumbakonam, Trichy-Vallam-Thanjavur-Thiruvaiyaru-Kumbakonam, 200, 22.7, 8.8, 15-02-2020 08:30 PM, 78, 84, 80, 71, 80, 108, 119, 109, 105

Trichy, Kumbakonam, Trichy-Lalgudi-Thanjavur-Thirukkarugavur-Kumb akonam, 200, 22.7, 8.8, 15-02-2020 08:35 PM, 45, 22, 49, 29, 27, 41, 44, 28, 54

Kumbakonam, Madurai, Kumbakonam-Ayyampettai-Thanjavur-Kallanai-Tri chy-Dindigul-Madurai, 280, 22.7, 12.3, 15-02-2020 08:45 PM, 18, 69, 40, 30, 41, 50, 50, 27, 99

Thanjavur, Trichy, Thanjavur-Kallanai-Trichy, 120, 22.7, 5.3, 15-02-2020 08:50 PM, 10, 24, 82, 76, 41, 94, 96, 15, 45

Kumbakonam, Trichy, Kumbakonam-Thiruvaiyaru-Thanjavur-Vallam-Trichy, 200, 22.7, 8.8, 15-02-2020 09:00 PM, 93, 82, 109, 113, 73, 119, 95, 113, 76

Madurai, Kumbakonam, Madurai-Puthukkottai-Trichy-Vallam-Thanjavur-Thiruvaiyaru-Kumbakonam, 280, 22.7, 12.3, 15-02-2020 09:10 PM, 87, 97, 113, 108, 78, 107, 83, 115, 108

Trichy, Kumbakonam, Trichy-Vallam-Thanjavur-Thiruvaiyaru-Kumbakonam, 200, 22.7, 8.8, 15-02-2020 09:20 PM, 78, 84, 80, 71, 80, 108, 119, 101, 103

Trichy, Kumbakonam, Trichy-Lalgudi-Thanjavur-Thirukkarugavur-Kumb akonam, 200, 22.7, 8.8, 15-02-2020 09:35 PM, 45, 22, 49, 29, 29, 41, 44, 28, 44

Kumbakonam, Madurai, Kumbakonam-Ayyampettai-Thanjavur-Kallanai-Tri chy-Dindigul-Madurai, 280, 22.7, 12.3, 15-02-2020 09:45 PM, 18, 69, 40, 30, 41, 50, 50, 28, 95

Thanjavur, Trichy, Thanjavur-Kallanai-Trichy, 120, 22.7, 5.3, 15-02-2020 09:55 PM, 10, 24, 82, 76, 41, 94, 90, 15, 45

Kumbakonam, Trichy, Kumbakonam-Thiruvaiyaru-Thanjavur-Vallam-Trichy, 200, 22.7, 8.8, 15-02-2020 10:00 PM, 93, 82, 109, 113, 73, 119, 95, 113, 76

Madurai, Kumbakonam, Madurai-Puthukkottai-Trichy-Vallam-Thanjavur-Thiruvaiyaru-Kumbakonam, 280, 22.7, 12.3, 15-02-2020 10:10 PM, 87, 97, 113, 108, 78, 107, 83, 115, 108

Kumbakonam, Madurai, Kumbakonam-Thiruvaiyaru-Thanjavur-Vallam-Tric hy-Puthukkottai-Madurai, 280, 22.7, 12.3, 15-02-2020 10:30 PM, 12, 26, 68, 52, 43, 20, 80, 96, 25

Thanjavur, Trichy, Thanjavur-Vallam-Trichy, 120, 22.7, 5.3, 15-02-2020 10:45 PM, 52, 46, 28, 73, 96, 74, 31, 94, 92

Thanjavur, Madurai, Thanjavur-Vallam-Trichy-Puthukkottai-Madurai, 210, 22.7, 8.8, 15-02-2020 10:50 PM, 81, 94, 98, 74, 116, 91, 93, 74, 65

Madurai, Trichy, Madurai-Puthukkottai-Trichy, 120, 22.7, 5.3, 15-02-2020 11:00 PM, 88, 70, 80, 107, 114, 108, 72, 80, 78

Trichy, Kumbakonam, Trichy-Vallam-Thanjavur-Thiruvaiyaru-Kumbakonam, 200, 22.7, 8.8, 15-02-2020 11:10 PM, 78, 84, 80, 71, 80, 108, 119, 90, 75

Trichy, Kumbakonam, Trichy-Lalgudi-Thanjavur-Thirukkarugavur-Kumb akonam, 200, 22.7, 8.8, 15-02-2020 11:25 PM, 45, 22, 49, 29, 27, 41, 44, 28, 54

Kumbakonam, Madurai, Kumbakonam-Ayyampettai-Thanjavur-Kallanai-Tri chy-Dindigul-Madurai, 280, 22.7, 12.3, 16-02-2020 08:00 AM, 18, 69, 40, 30, 41, 50, 50, 27, 99

Thanjavur, Trichy, Thanjavur-Kallanai-Trichy, 120, 22.7, 5.3, 16-02-2020 08:20 PM, 10, 24, 82, 76, 41, 94, 96, 15, 55

Kumbakonam, Trichy, Kumbakonam-Thiruvaiyaru-Thanjavur-Vallam-Trichy, 200, 22.7, 8.8, 16-02-2020 08:35 PM, 93, 82, 109, 113, 73, 119, 95, 103, 74

Madurai, Kumbakonam, Madurai-Puthukkottai-Trichy-Vallam-Thanjavur-Thiruvaiyaru-Kumbakonam, 280, 22.7, 12.3, 16-02-2020 08:45 PM, 87, 97, 113, 108, 78, 107, 83, 115, 100

Kumbakonam, Madurai, Kumbakonam-Thiruvaiyaru-Thanjavur-Vallam-Tric hy-Puthukkottai-Madurai, 280, 22.7, 12.3, 16-02-2020 09:00 PM, 12, 26, 68, 52, 43, 20, 80, 96, 25

Thanjavur, Trichy, Thanjavur-Vallam-Trichy, 120, 22.7, 5.3, 16-02-2020 09:10 PM, 52, 46, 28, 73, 96, 74, 31, 94, 91

Thanjavur, Madurai, Thanjavur-Vallam-Trichy-Puthukkottai-Madurai, 210, 22.7, 8.8, 16-02-2020 10:50 PM, 81, 94, 98, 74, 116, 91, 93, 74, 60

Madurai, Trichy, Madurai-Puthukkottai-Trichy, 120, 22.7, 5.3, 16-02-2020 11:00 PM, 88, 70, 80, 110, 114, 108, 70, 80, 68

Trichy, Kumbakonam, Trichy-Vallam-Thanjavur-Thiruvaiyaru-Kumbakonam, 200, 22.7, 8.8, 16-02-2020 11:30 PM, 78, 84, 80, 71, 80, 108, 119, 90, 75

Trichy, Kumbakonam, Trichy-Lalgudi-Thanjavur-Thirukkarugavur-Kumb akonam, 200, 22.7, 8.8, 17-02-2020 08:05 AM, 45, 22, 49, 29, 27, 41, 44, 28, 54

Kumbakonam, Madurai, Kumbakonam-Ayyampettai-Thanjavur-Kallanai-Tri chy-Dindigul-Madurai, 280, 22.7, 12.3, 17-02-2020 08:25 AM, 18, 69, 40, 30, 41, 50, 50, 27, 99

Thanjavur, Trichy, Thanjavur-Kallanai-Trichy, 120, 22.7, 5.3, 17-02-2020 08:45 AM, 10, 24, 82, 76, 41, 94, 96, 15, 50

Kumbakonam, Trichy, Kumbakonam-Thiruvaiyaru-Thanjavur-Vallam-Trichy, 200, 22.7, 8.8, 17-02-2020 09:00 AM, 93, 82, 109, 113, 73, 119, 95, 104, 78

Madurai, Kumbakonam, Madurai-Puthukkottai-Trichy-Vallam-Thanjavur-Thiruvaiyaru-Kumbakonam, 280, 22.7, 12.3, 17-02-2020 09:15 AM, 87, 97, 113, 108, 78, 107, 83, 115, 100

Thanjavur, Madurai, Thanjavur-Vallam-Trichy-Puthukkottai-Madurai, 210, 22.7, 8.8, 17-02-2020 09:35 AM, 81, 94, 98, 74, 116, 91, 93, 74, 60

Madurai, Trichy, Madurai-Puthukkottai-Trichy, 120, 22.7, 5.3, 17-02-2020 09:50 AM, 88, 70, 80, 110, 114, 108, 70, 80, 68

Trichy, Kumbakonam, Trichy-Vallam-Thanjavur-Thiruvaiyaru-Kumbakonam, 200, 22.7, 8.8, 17-02-2020 10:00 AM, 78, 84, 80, 71, 80, 108, 119, 90, 75

Trichy, Kumbakonam, Trichy-Lalgudi-Thanjavur-Thirukkarugavur-Kumb akonam, 200, 22.7, 8.8, 17-02-2020 10:15 AM, 45, 22, 49, 29, 27, 41, 44, 28, 54

Kumbakonam, Madurai, Kumbakonam-Ayyampettai-Thanjavur-Kallanai-Tri chy-Dindigul-Madurai, 280, 22.7, 12.3, 17-02-2020 10:35 AM, 18, 69, 40, 30, 41, 50, 50, 27, 99

Thanjavur, Trichy, Thanjavur-Kallanai-Trichy, 120, 22.7, 5.3, 17-02-2020 11:00 AM, 10, 24, 82, 76, 41, 94, 96, 15, 50

Kumbakonam, Trichy, Kumbakonam-Thiruvaiyaru-Thanjavur-Vallam-Trichy, 200, 22.7, 8.8, 17-02-2020 11:15 AM, 93, 82, 109, 113, 73, 119, 95, 104, 78

Madurai, Kumbakonam, Madurai-Puthukkottai-Trichy-Vallam-Thanjavur-Thiruvaiyaru-Kumbakonam, 280, 22.7, 12.3, 17-02-2020 11:30 AM, 87, 97, 113, 108, 78, 107, 83, 115, 100

Trichy, Kumbakonam, Trichy-Lalgudi-Thanjavur-Thirukkarugavur-Kumb akonam, 200, 22.7, 8.8, 17-02-2020 11:45 AM, 45, 22, 49, 29, 27, 41, 44, 28, 54

Kumbakonam, Madurai, Kumbakonam-Ayyampettai-Thanjavur-Kallanai-Tri chy-Dindigul-Madurai, 280, 22.7, 12.3, 17-02-2020 04:00 PM, 18, 69, 40, 30, 41, 50, 50, 27, 99

Thanjavur, Trichy, Thanjavur-Kallanai-Trichy, 120, 22.7, 5.3, 17-02-2020 04:20 PM, 10, 24, 82, 76, 41, 94, 96, 15, 55

Kumbakonam, Trichy, Kumbakonam-Thiruvaiyaru-Thanjavur-Vallam-Trichy, 200, 22.7, 8.8, 17-02-2020 04:35 PM, 93, 82, 109, 113, 73, 119, 95, 103, 74

Madurai, Kumbakonam, Madurai-Puthukkottai-Trichy-Vallam-Thanjavur-Thiruvaiyaru-Kumbakonam, 280, 22.7, 12.3, 17-02-2020 04:45 PM, 87, 97, 113, 108, 78, 107, 83, 115, 100

Kumbakonam, Madurai, Kumbakonam-Thiruvaiyaru-Thanjavur-Vallam-Tric hy-Puthukkottai-Madurai, 280, 22.7, 12.3, 17-02-2020 05:00 PM, 12, 26, 68, 52, 43, 20, 80, 96, 25

Thanjavur, Trichy, Thanjavur-Vallam-Trichy, 120, 22.7, 5.3, 17-02-2020 05:10 PM, 52, 46, 28, 73, 96, 74, 31, 94, 91

Thanjavur, Madurai, Thanjavur-Vallam-Trichy-Puthukkottai-Madurai, 210, 22.7, 8.8, 17-02-2020 05:35 PM, 81, 94, 98, 74, 116, 91, 93, 74, 60

Madurai, Trichy, Madurai-Puthukkottai-Trichy, 120, 22.7, 5.3, 17-02-2020 05:45 PM, 88, 70, 80, 110, 114, 108, 70, 80, 68

Trichy, Kumbakonam, Trichy-Vallam-Thanjavur-Thiruvaiyaru-Kumbakonam, 200, 22.7, 8.8, 17-02-2020 06:00 PM, 78, 84, 80, 71, 80, 108, 119, 90, 75

Trichy, Kumbakonam, Trichy-Lalgudi-Thanjavur-Thirukkarugavur-Kumb akonam, 200, 22.7, 8.8, 17-02-2020 06:15 PM, 45, 22, 49, 29, 27, 41, 44, 28, 54

Kumbakonam, Madurai, Kumbakonam-Ayyampettai-Thanjavur-Kallanai-Tri chy-Dindigul-Madurai, 280, 22.7, 12.3, 17-02-2020 06:25 PM, 18, 69, 40, 30, 41, 50, 50, 27, 99

Thanjavur, Trichy, Thanjavur-Kallanai-Trichy, 120, 22.7, 5.3, 17-02-2020 06:45 PM, 10, 24, 82, 76, 41, 94, 96, 15, 50

Kumbakonam, Trichy, Kumbakonam-Thiruvaiyaru-Thanjavur-Vallam-Trichy, 200, 22.7, 8.8, 17-02-2020 07:00 PM, 93, 82, 109, 113, 73, 119, 95, 104, 78

Madurai, Kumbakonam, Madurai-Puthukkottai-Trichy-Vallam-Thanjavur-Thiruvaiyaru-Kumbakonam, 280, 22.7, 12.3, 17-02-2020 07:15 PM, 87, 97, 113, 108, 78, 107, 83, 115, 100

Thanjavur, Madurai, Thanjavur-Vallam-Trichy-Puthukkottai-Madurai, 210, 22.7, 8.8, 17-02-2020 07:35 PM, 81, 94, 98, 74, 116, 91, 93, 74, 60

Madurai, Trichy, Madurai-Puthukkottai-Trichy, 120, 22.7, 5.3, 17-02-2020 07:50 PM, 88, 70, 80, 110, 114, 108, 70, 80, 68

Trichy, Kumbakonam, Trichy-Vallam-Thanjavur-Thiruvaiyaru-Kumbakonam, 200, 22.7, 8.8, 17-02-2020 08:00 PM, 78, 84, 80, 71, 80, 108, 119, 90, 75

Trichy, Kumbakonam, Trichy-Lalgudi-Thanjavur-Thirukkarugavur-Kumb akonam, 200, 22.7, 8.8, 17-02-2020 08:15 PM, 45, 22, 49, 29, 27, 41, 44, 28, 54

Kumbakonam, Madurai, Kumbakonam-Ayyampettai-Thanjavur-Kallanai-Tri chy-Dindigul-Madurai, 280, 22.7, 12.3, 17-02-2020 08:35 PM, 18, 69, 40, 30, 41, 50, 50, 27, 99

Thanjavur, Trichy, Thanjavur-Kallanai-Trichy, 120, 22.7, 5.3, 17-02-2020 08:45 PM, 10, 24, 82, 76, 41, 94, 96, 15, 50

Kumbakonam, Trichy, Kumbakonam-Thiruvaiyaru-Thanjavur-Vallam-Trichy, 200, 22.7, 8.8, 17-02-2020 08:55 PM, 93, 82, 109, 113, 73, 119, 95, 104, 78

Madurai, Kumbakonam, Madurai-Puthukkottai-Trichy-Vallam-Thanjavur-Thiruvaiyaru-Kumbakonam, 280, 22.7, 12.3, 17-02-2020 09:00 PM, 87, 97, 113, 108, 78, 107, 83, 115, 100

A sample dataset is shown above. The algorithm uses TPCA clustering algorithms to achieve this, as demonstrated below. It separates the dataset into clusters based on each location.

CLUSTERED DATASET

KUMBAKONAM

Kumbakonam, Madurai, Kumbakonam-Thiruvaiyaru-Thanjavur-Vallam-Tric hy-Puthukkottai-Madurai, 280, 22.7, 12.3, 14-02-2020 09:45 PM, 12, 26, 68, 52, 53, 10, 90, 59, 25

Kumbakonam, Madurai, Kumbakonam-Ayyampettai-Thanjavur-Kallanai-Tri chy-Dindigul-Madurai, 280, 22.7, 12.3, 14-02-2020 09:45 PM, 18, 69, 40, 30, 41, 50, 50, 27, 99

Kumbakonam, Trichy, Kumbakonam-Thiruvaiyaru-Thanjavur-Vallam-Trichy, 200, 22.7, 8.8, 15-02-2020 05:15 PM, 93, 82, 109, 113, 73, 119, 95, 113, 76

Kumbakonam, Madurai, Kumbakonam-Thiruvaiyaru-Thanjavur-Vallam-Tric hy-Puthukkottai-Madurai, 280, 22.7, 12.3, 15-02-2020 05:45 PM, 12, 26, 68, 52, 43, 20, 90, 69, 25

Kumbakonam, Madurai, Kumbakonam-Ayyampettai-Thanjavur-Kallanai-Trichy-Dindigul-Madurai, 280, 22.7, 12.3, 15-02-2020 08:45 PM, 18, 69, 40, 30, 41, 50, 50, 27, 99

Kumbakonam, Trichy, Kumbakonam-Thiruvaiyaru-Thanjavur-Vallam-Trichy, 200, 22.7, 8.8, 15-02-2020 09:00 PM, 93, 82, 109, 113, 73, 119, 95, 113, 76

Kumbakonam, Madurai, Kumbakonam-Ayyampettai-Thanjavur-Kallanai-Trichy-Dindigul-Madurai, 280, 22.7, 12.3, 15-02-2020 09:45 PM, 18, 69, 40, 30, 41, 50, 50, 28, 95

Kumbakonam, Trichy, Kumbakonam-Thiruvaiyaru-Thanjavur-Vallam-Trichy, 200, 22.7, 8.8, 15-02-2020 10:00 PM, 93, 82, 109, 113, 73, 119, 95, 113, 76

Kumbakonam, Madurai, Kumbakonam-Thiruvaiyaru-Thanjavur-Vallam-Trichy-Puthukkottai-Madurai, 280, 22.7, 12.3, 15-02-2020 10:30 PM, 12, 26, 68, 52, 43, 20, 80, 96, 25

Kumbakonam, Madurai, Kumbakonam-Ayyampettai-Thanjavur-Kallanai-Trichy-Dindigul-Madurai, 280, 22.7, 12.3, 16-02-2020 08:00 AM, 18, 69, 40, 30, 41, 50, 50, 27, 99

Kumbakonam, Madurai, Kumbakonam-Thiruvaiyaru-Thanjavur-Vallam-Trichy-Puthukkottai-Madurai, 280, 22.7, 12.3, 16-02-2020 09:00 PM, 12, 26, 68, 52, 43, 20, 80, 96, 25

Kumbakonam, Madurai, Kumbakonam-Ayyampettai-Thanjavur-Kallanai-Trichy-Dindigul-Madurai, 280, 22.7, 12.3, 17-02-2020 08:25 AM, 18, 69, 40, 30, 41, 50, 50, 27, 99

Kumbakonam, Trichy, Kumbakonam-Thiruvaiyaru-Thanjavur-Vallam-Trichy, 200, 22.7, 8.8, 17-02-2020 09:00 AM, 93, 82, 109, 113, 73, 119, 95, 104, 78

Kumbakonam, Madurai, Kumbakonam-Ayyampettai-Thanjavur-Kallanai-Trichy-Dindigul-Madurai, 280, 22.7, 12.3, 17-02-2020 10:35 AM, 18, 69, 40, 30, 41, 50, 50, 27, 99

Kumbakonam, Trichy, Kumbakonam-Thiruvaiyaru-Thanjavur-Vallam-Trichy, 200, 22.7, 8.8, 17-02-2020 11:15 AM, 93, 82, 109, 113, 73, 119, 95, 104, 78

Kumbakonam, Madurai, Kumbakonam-Ayyampettai-Thanjavur-Kallanai-Trichy-Dindigul-Madurai, 280, 22.7, 12.3, 17-02-2020 04:00 PM, 18, 69, 40, 30, 41, 50, 50, 27, 99

Kumbakonam, Trichy, Kumbakonam-Thiruvaiyaru-Thanjavur-Vallam-Trichy, 200, 22.7, 8.8, 17-02-2020 04:35 PM, 93, 82, 109, 113, 73, 119, 95, 103, 74

Kumbakonam, Madurai, Kumbakonam-Thiruvaiyaru-Thanjavur-Vallam-Trichy-Puthukkottai-Madurai, 280, 22.7, 12.3, 17-02-2020 05:00 PM, 12, 26, 68, 52, 43, 20, 80, 96, 25

Kumbakonam, Madurai, Kumbakonam-Ayyampettai-Thanjavur-Kallanai-Trichy-Dindigul-Madurai, 280, 22.7, 12.3, 17-02-2020 06:25 PM, 18, 69, 40, 30, 41, 50, 50, 27, 99

Kumbakonam, Trichy, Kumbakonam-Thiruvaiyaru-Thanjavur-Vallam-Trichy, 200, 22.7, 8.8, 17-02-2020 07:00 PM, 93, 82, 109, 113, 73, 119, 95, 104, 78

Kumbakonam, Madurai, Kumbakonam-Ayyampettai-Thanjavur-Kallanai-Trichy-Dindigul-Madurai, 280, 22.7, 12.3, 17-02-2020 08:35 PM, 18, 69, 40, 30, 41, 50, 50, 27, 99

Kumbakonam, Trichy, Kumbakonam-Thiruvaiyaru-Thanjavur-Vallam-Trichy, 200, 22.7, 8.8, 17-02-2020 08:55 PM, 93, 82, 109, 113, 73, 119, 95, 104, 78

TRICHY

Trichy, Kumbakonam, Trichy-Vallam-Thanjavur-Thiruvaiyaru-Kumbakonam, 200, 22.7, 8.8, 15-02-2020 08:00 AM, 1, 1, 1, 1, 1, 1, 1, 1, 1, 1, Heavy_Traffic

Trichy, Kumbakonam, Trichy-Lalgudi-Thanjavur-Thirukkarugavur-Kumbakonam, 200, 22.7, 8.8, 14-02-2020 09:55 PM, 0, 0, 0, 0, 0, 0, 0, 0, 0, 0, Normal

Trichy, Kumbakonam, Trichy-Vallam-Thanjavur-Thiruvaiyaru-Kumbakonam, 200, 22.7, 8.8, 15-02-2020 08:30 PM, 78, 84, 80, 71, 80, 108, 119, 109, 105

Trichy, Kumbakonam, Trichy-Lalgudi-Thanjavur-Thirukkarugavur-Kumbakonam, 200, 22.7, 8.8, 15-02-2020 08:35 PM, 45, 22, 49, 29, 27, 41, 44, 28, 54

Trichy, Kumbakonam, Trichy-Vallam-Thanjavur-Thiruvaiyaru-Kumbakonam, 200, 22.7, 8.8, 15-02-2020 09:20 PM, 78, 84, 80, 71, 80, 108, 119, 101, 103

Trichy, Kumbakonam, Trichy-Lalgudi-Thanjavur-Thirukkarugavur-Kumbakonam, 200, 22.7, 8.8, 15-02-2020 09:35 PM, 45, 22, 49, 29, 29, 41, 44, 28, 44

Trichy, Kumbakonam, Trichy-Vallam-Thanjavur-Thiruvaiyaru-Kumbakonam, 200, 22.7, 8.8, 15-02-2020 11:10 PM, 78, 84, 80, 71, 80, 108, 119, 90, 75

Trichy, Kumbakonam, Trichy-Lalgudi-Thanjavur-Thirukkarugavur-Kumbakonam, 200, 22.7, 8.8, 15-02-2020 11:25 PM, 45, 22, 49, 29, 27, 41, 44, 28, 54

Trichy, Kumbakonam, Trichy-Vallam-Thanjavur-Thiruvaiyaru-Kumbakonam, 200, 22.7, 8.8, 16-02-2020 11:30 PM, 78, 84, 80, 71, 80, 108, 119, 90, 75

Trichy, Kumbakonam, Trichy-Lalgudi-Thanjavur-Thirukkarugavur-Kumbakonam, 200, 22.7, 8.8, 17-02-2020 08:05 AM, 45, 22, 49, 29, 27, 41, 44, 28, 54

Trichy, Kumbakonam, Trichy-Vallam-Thanjavur-Thiruvaiyaru-Kumbakonam, 200, 22.7, 8.8, 17-02-2020 10:00 AM, 78, 84, 80, 71, 80, 108, 119, 90, 75

Trichy, Kumbakonam, Trichy-Lalgudi-Thanjavur-Thirukkarugavur-Kumbakonam, 200, 22.7, 8.8, 17-02-2020 10:15AM, 45, 22, 49, 29, 27, 41, 44, 28, 54

Trichy, Kumbakonam, Trichy-Vallam-Thanjavur-Thiruvaiyaru-Kumbakonam, 200, 22.7, 8.8, 17-02-2020 08:00 PM, 78, 84, 80, 71, 80, 108, 119, 90, 75

Trichy, Kumbakonam, Trichy-Lalgudi-Thanjavur-Thirukkarugavur-Kumbakonam, 200, 22.7, 8.8, 17-02-2020 08:15PM, 45, 22, 49, 29, 27, 41, 44, 28, 54

Kumbakonam, Madurai, Kumbakonam-Thiruvaiyaru-Thanjavur-Vallam-Trichy-Puthukkottai-Madurai, 280, 22.7, 12.3, 16-02-2020 09:00 PM, 12, 26, 68, 52, 43, 20, 80, 96, 25

Kumbakonam, Madurai, Kumbakonam-Ayyampettai-Thanjavur-Kallanai-Trichy-Dindigul-Madurai, 280, 22.7, 12.3, 17-02-2020 08:25 AM, 18, 69, 40, 30, 41, 50, 50, 27, 99

Kumbakonam, Trichy, Kumbakonam-Thiruvaiyaru-Thanjavur-Vallam-Trichy, 200, 22.7, 8.8, 17-02-2020 09:00 AM, 93, 82, 109, 113, 73, 119, 95, 104, 78

Kumbakonam, Madurai, Kumbakonam-Ayyampettai-Thanjavur-Kallanai-Trichy-Dindigul-Madurai, 280, 22.7, 12.3, 17-02-2020 10:35 AM, 18, 69, 40, 30, 41, 50, 50, 27, 99

Kumbakonam, Trichy, Kumbakonam-Thiruvaiyaru-Thanjavur-Vallam-Trichy, 200, 22.7, 8.8, 17-02-2020 11:15 AM, 93, 82, 109, 113, 73, 119, 95, 104, 78

Kumbakonam, Madurai, Kumbakonam-Ayyampettai-Thanjavur-Kallanai-Trichy-Dindigul-Madurai, 280, 22.7, 12.3, 17-02-2020 04:00 PM, 18, 69, 40, 30, 41, 50, 50, 27, 99

Kumbakonam, Trichy, Kumbakonam-Thiruvaiyaru-Thanjavur-Vallam-Trichy, 200, 22.7, 8.8, 17-02-2020 04:35 PM, 93, 82, 109, 113, 73, 119, 95, 103, 74

Kumbakonam, Madurai, Kumbakonam-Thiruvaiyaru-Thanjavur-Vallam-Trichy-Puthukkottai-Madurai, 280, 22.7, 12.3, 17-02-2020 05:00 PM, 12, 26, 68, 52, 43, 20, 80, 96, 25

Kumbakonam, Madurai, Kumbakonam-Ayyampettai-Thanjavur-Kallanai-Trichy-Dindigul-Madurai, 280, 22.7, 12.3, 17-02-2020 06:25 PM, 18, 69, 40, 30, 41, 50, 50, 27, 99

Kumbakonam, Trichy, Kumbakonam-Thiruvaiyaru-Thanjavur-Vallam-Trichy, 200, 22.7, 8.8, 17-02-2020 07:00 PM, 93, 82, 109, 113, 73, 119, 95, 104, 78

Kumbakonam, Madurai, Kumbakonam-Ayyampettai-Thanjavur-Kallanai-Trichy-Dindigul-Madurai, 280, 22.7, 12.3, 17-02-2020 08:35 PM, 18, 69, 40, 30, 41, 50, 50, 27, 99

Kumbakonam, Trichy, Kumbakonam-Thiruvaiyaru-Thanjavur-Vallam-Trichy, 200, 22.7, 8.8, 17-02-2020 08:55 PM, 93, 82, 109, 113, 73, 119, 95, 104, 78

TRICHY

Trichy, Kumbakonam, Trichy-Vallam-Thanjavur-Thiruvaiyaru-Kumbakonam, 200, 22.7, 8.8, 15-02-2020 08:00 AM, 1, 1, 1, 1, 1, 1, 1, 1, 1, 1, Heavy_Traffic

Trichy, Kumbakonam, Trichy-Lalgudi-Thanjavur-Thirukkarugavur-Kumbakonam, 200, 22.7, 8.8, 14-02-2020 09:55 PM, 0, 0, 0, 0, 0, 0, 0, 0, 0, 0, Normal

Trichy, Kumbakonam, Trichy-Vallam-Thanjavur-Thiruvaiyaru-Kumbakonam, 200, 22.7, 8.8, 15-02-2020 08:30 PM, 78, 84, 80, 71, 80, 108, 119, 109, 105

Trichy, Kumbakonam, Trichy-Lalgudi-Thanjavur-Thirukkarugavur-Kumbakonam, 200, 22.7, 8.8, 15-02-2020 08:35 PM, 45, 22, 49, 29, 27, 41, 44, 28, 54

Trichy, Kumbakonam, Trichy-Vallam-Thanjavur-Thiruvaiyaru-Kumbakonam, 200, 22.7, 8.8, 15-02-2020 09:20 PM, 78, 84, 80, 71, 80, 108, 119, 101, 103

Trichy, Kumbakonam, Trichy-Lalgudi-Thanjavur-Thirukkarugavur-Kumbakonam, 200, 22.7, 8.8, 15-02-2020 09:35 PM, 45, 22, 49, 29, 29, 41, 44, 28, 44

Trichy, Kumbakonam, Trichy-Vallam-Thanjavur-Thiruvaiyaru-Kumbakonam, 200, 22.7, 8.8, 15-02-2020 11:10 PM, 78, 84, 80, 71, 80, 108, 119, 90, 75

Trichy, Kumbakonam, Trichy-Lalgudi-Thanjavur-Thirukkarugavur-Kumbakonam, 200, 22.7, 8.8, 15-02-2020 11:25 PM, 45, 22, 49, 29, 27, 41, 44, 28, 54

Trichy, Kumbakonam, Trichy-Vallam-Thanjavur-Thiruvaiyaru-Kumbakonam, 200, 22.7, 8.8, 16-02-2020 11:30 PM, 78, 84, 80, 71, 80, 108, 119, 90, 75

Trichy, Kumbakonam, Trichy-Lalgudi-Thanjavur-Thirukkarugavur-Kumb akonam, 200, 22.7, 8.8, 17-02-2020 08:05 AM, 45, 22, 49, 29, 27, 41, 44, 28, 54

Trichy, Kumbakonam, Trichy-Vallam-Thanjavur-Thiruvaiyaru-Kumbakonam, 200, 22.7, 8.8, 17-02-2020 10:00 AM, 78, 84, 80, 71, 80, 108, 119, 90, 75

Trichy, Kumbakonam, Trichy-Lalgudi-Thanjavur-Thirukkarugavur-Kumb akonam, 200, 22.7, 8.8, 17-02-2020 10:15AM, 45, 22, 49, 29, 27, 41, 44, 28, 54

Trichy, Kumbakonam, Trichy-Vallam-Thanjavur-Thiruvaiyaru-Kumbakonam, 200, 22.7, 8.8, 17-02-2020 08:00 PM, 78, 84, 80, 71, 80, 108, 119, 90, 75

Trichy, Kumbakonam, Trichy-Lalgudi-Thanjavur-Thirukkarugavur-Kumb akonam, 200, 22.7, 8.8, 17-02-2020 08:15PM, 45, 22, 49, 29, 27, 41, 44, 28, 54

Figure 3.5 shows the calculated congestion level and congestion status for each instance (rows). If the congestion level is above 0.40, it will show that the congestion status is Heavy_ Traffic. Otherwise, it shows normal. This figure concludes that during peak hours (07.00 AM–09.00 AM and 05.00 PM–07.00 PM), the congestion level rises to above 0.40. Therefore, each location suffers from heavy traffic in peak hours. Table 3.4 shows the congestion level and congestion status of Madurai City from the traffic flow dataset after the TPCA with modified FCM algorithm is applied.

Furthermore, traffic prediction and congestion avoidance are shown in Figure 3.6. This shows the predicted traffic between Thanjavur and Madurai. It calculates the congestion level on all available routes between a source location and a destination location. Then, the best route is recommended to the user.

Figure 3.7 shows traffic prediction and congestion avoidance during peak hours. Less congested routes are then recommended to the user. Chennai is one of the cities in India that is connected by the Golden Quadrilateral system of National Highways. It is connected to four major national highways (NH) that originate in the city. Even with facilitated road transport, Chennai is facing major traffic issues both into and out of the city.

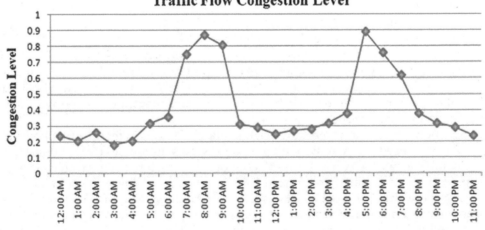

FIGURE 3.5
Congestion level.

TABLE 3.4

Madurai City Traffic Congestion Level and Congestion Status

Time	Congestion Level	Congestion Status
12.00 AM	0.24	Normal
1.00 AM	0.21	Normal
2.00 AM	0.26	Normal
3.00 AM	0.18	Normal
4.00 AM	0.21	Normal
5.00 AM	0.32	Normal
6.00 AM	0.36	Normal
7.00 AM	0.75	Heavy Traffic
8.00 AM	0.87	Heavy Traffic
9.00 AM	0.81	Heavy Traffic
10.00 AM	0.31	Normal
11.00 AM	0.29	Normal
12.00 PM	0.25	Normal
1.00 PM	0.27	Normal
2.00 PM	0.28	Normal
3.00 PM	0.32	Normal
4.00 PM	0.38	Normal
5.00 PM	0.89	Heavy Traffic
6.00 PM	0.76	Heavy Traffic
7.00 PM	0.62	Heavy Traffic
8.00 PM	0.38	Normal
9.00 PM	0.32	Normal
10.00 PM	0.29	Normal
11.00 PM	0.24	Normal

There is not a single place in Chennai without traffic. Thirty-one stretches across the city are considered dangerous. The top black spot areas which have the worst traffic conditions are given in Table 3.5.

Chennai is all set to get an "intelligent transportation system" covering at least 150 junctions with financial aid from the Japan International Cooperation Agency (JICA). The smart transport system aims at offering commuters comfortable, reliable, quick, affordable, and safe access. It is unable to rationalize the signal timings based on traffic volume at the junction level, but the Chennai City Traffic Police (CCTP) is considering a grid of traffic signals that can communicate with each other and ensure the smoothest possible flow of traffic within a particular zone.

Table 3.5 shows the most important black spots in Chennai where traffic congestion persists. The proposed S-TPCA system aims to provide solutions to traffic congestion in these vulnerable areas. We consider one black spot area which has more traffic congestion during peak hours: the traffic route from Saidapet to George Town. Most vehicles tend to be heading towards Saidapet as this is the main center of the city. This route passes via Nungambakkam and T. Nagar, and it is one of the busiest routes in Chennai. During weekends and holidays, these places become more crowded with vehicles as people tend to leave the city. To avoid traffic congestion, we count the number of vehicles arriving at a particular time. Based on probability, if the vehicle count is high, then an alert can be

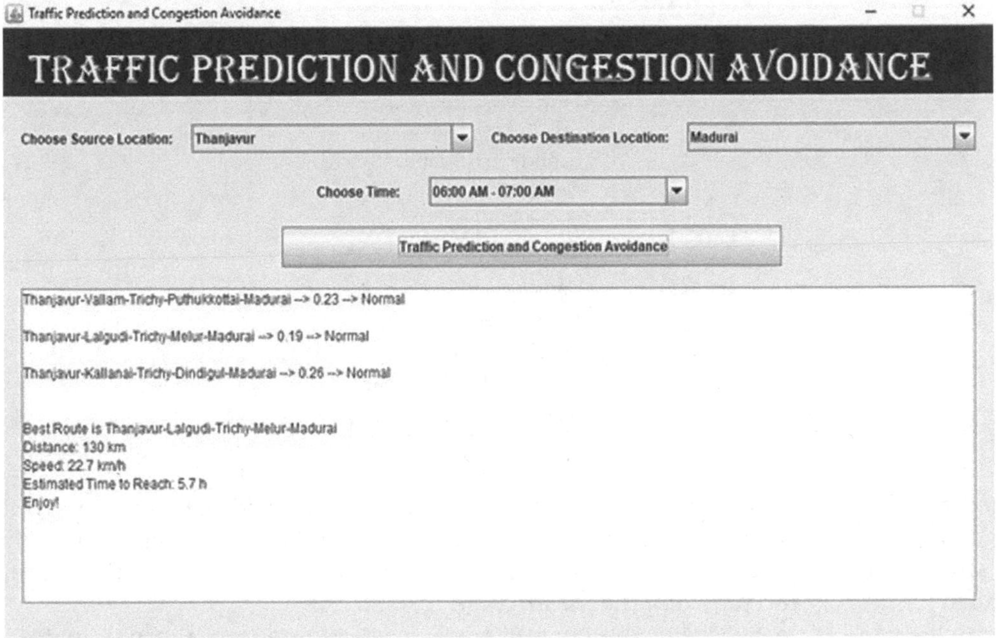

FIGURE 3.6
Traffic predictions and congestion avoidance.

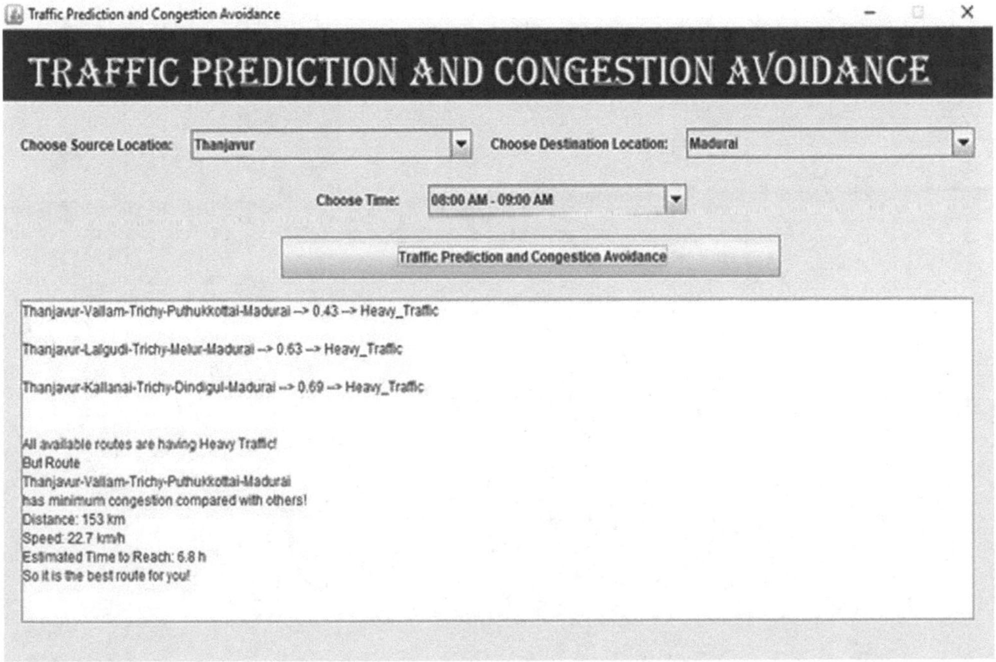

FIGURE 3.7
Traffic predictions and congestion avoidance during peak hours.

TABLE 3.5

Top Black Spot Areas in Chennai

S. No.	Place
1.	TIDEL Park signal
2.	Guindy to Saidapet stretch
3.	Adyar
4.	Vadapalani signal
5.	Velachery
6.	Usman Road
7.	Teynampet
8.	Marina Beach Road
9.	Jawaharlal Nehru Road
10.	Meenambakkam

issued to take alternative paths to reach the destination and avoid encountering traffic. The distance might be slightly greater but time and fuel can be saved; thereby pollution can also be controlled and the environment can be protected. We have shown the alternate paths in Figure. 3.8 and provided the information in Table 3.6.

Vehicles can be alerted about the current traffic scenario and an alternate path can be chosen to avoid traffic and also to save time and fuel. The dataset collection for analyzing the traffic is done manually for the first two weeks of August, taking the historical background into consideration. Based on the proposed S-TPCA algorithm,

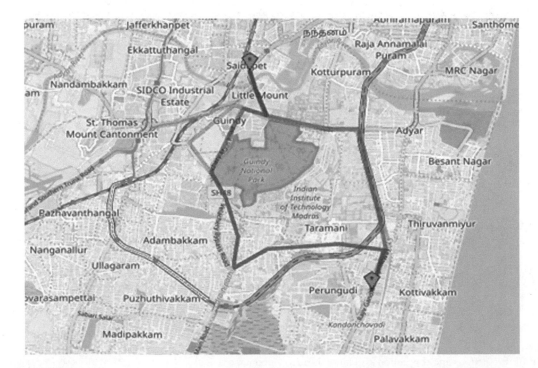

FIGURE 3.8
Alternate paths for travel.

TABLE 3.6

Alternate Route Details

Route Path			
Route ID	Route 1	Route 2	Route 3
Estimated time (min)	37	45	50
Distance (approx. km)	13.3	12.9	14
Estimated speed (kmph)	36–40	30–35	30–35

let us consider the average number of vehicles (m) on Route 1 from August 1 to August 15 to be 53,678,95. The vehicle distribution includes all two wheelers and four wheelers. The average speed (v) of the vehicles is calculated to be 40km/hr. The estimated travel time on Route 1 is found to be 10 minutes. The arrival interval for the vehicles is found to be 0.50 seconds. The time of arrival is judged based on the time period considered. Let us consider the traffic on Sundays between 5.00 PM and 7.00 PM. The arrival times of vehicles are distributed at intervals of 0.10 seconds from 5.00 to 7.00 PM. The values for the Poisson distribution are calculated with the suggested values in the following formula.

$$P(v) = \frac{m^v e^{-m}}{v!} = \frac{1}{v!}\left(\frac{Rt}{3600}\right)^{ve^{-\frac{vt}{3600}}} \tag{3.8}$$

The probability for Poisson distribution is found to be 0.8 by substituting the values in the above formula. Based on the arrival time interval, the membership function is calculated to be 0.6. Further applying this, the fitness value (f) is calculated to be 0.7. Further, after applying the proposed S-TPCA algorithm, the genetic function G takes the value of 0.6 and the fitness value (f′) is found to be 0.834. Since f′ is greater than f, the new updated value can be used to identify the traffic state.

The proposed TPCA system is compared to the conventional system A_m as referred to in Osorio and Nanduri (2015). The average arrival time is an important parameter which is taken as subject of comparison between the two models. The proposed system shows a better value of the cumulative distribution function compared to the existing system of traffic prediction.

In the traffic prediction system, the threshold value for determining the traffic congestion ranges from 0 to 1. On Route 1, the traffic is at its peak during the interval from 5.00 PM to 7.00 PM on Sundays. The observed threshold value during this interval on Route 1 is 0.85. This threshold is greater than 0.40, which is the moderate value for traffic that does not lead to congestion. Thus traffic through Route 1 is found to be high during this period. In a similar manner, traffic is predicted for the other routes, namely Route 2 and Route 3. Then the excess traffic on Route 1 is redirected via any other route for which the threshold value is nearer to 0.40.

Fuel consumption is also comparable, and the structure of the proposed system based on the arrival time proves to be efficient. The proposed TPCA system has the ability to avoid congestion and also enable smooth transportation. Figure 3.9 illustrates how the proposed technique compares in terms of average time interval. Figure 3.10 gives the comparison based on fuel consumption.

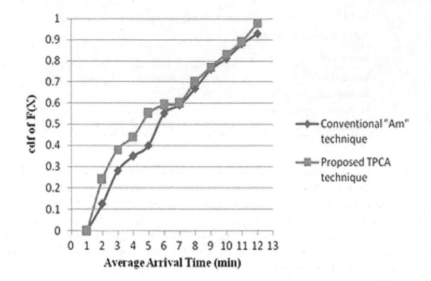

FIGURE 3.9
Comparison based on arrival time (min).

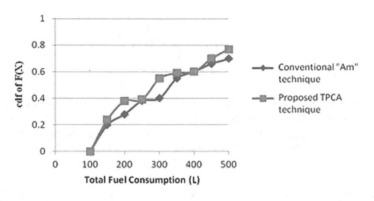

FIGURE 3.10
Comparison based on fuel consumption (L).

3.7 Summary

This work proposed a prediction and congestion avoidance technique based on genetic model traffic prediction. This work first obtains sample data on hourly volume in low and moderate recurring volume. It then established a probability model and genetic prediction model for predicting traffic congestion and avoidance. The results represent the experimental relation between observed frequency and predicted frequency. This prediction technique with a fuel consumption model helps to avoid congestion and also reduces pollution, protects the environment, and improves travel safety. The proposed solution can be applied in any of the metropolitan cities of India. The results show that a prediction method based on a mathematical genetic model is an effective approach for traffic flow prediction and congestion avoidance.

4

Short-Term Traffic Prediction Model (STTPM)

4.1 Introduction

In terms of growth in economy and population, India is the second largest country. Most cities in India are facing road congestion problems. There are practical difficulties in maintaining intelligent transport management systems (ITMS) in developed countries and metropolitan cities in India. This is due to the slow growth of infrastructure compared to the rapid increase in the number of vehicles and space and cost constraints. Traffic flow information is needed for travelers to help them to make better travel decisions concerning congestion and to improve traffic operation efficiency. Predicting short-term traffic flow will be more helpful in managing freeway networks.

4.2 Need for Traffic Flow Prediction

With the rapid increase in the number of vehicles and road traffic volume, which leads to serious traffic congestion and frequent accidents, how to solve this problem effectively is the research hotspot in terms of traffic control and traffic guidance systems. The system uses historical or current traffic flow data to predict the traffic situation at some period in the future, and to provide available information for traffic departments to implement traffic control and road guidance. It helps users choose the best road and reduces travel time to decrease traffic jams. So, short-term traffic prediction is used to control and guide traffic. At present there are many algorithms for short-term traffic flow prediction. Cui (2010) proposed several prediction models including cross traffic flow prediction, section traffic flow, and accident prediction. The early main algorithms are autoregressive (AR), moving average (MA), auto regressive moving average (ARMA), history average (HA), and the BoxCox method. With further research, many more complex and more precise models have been presented. There are two kinds of models; one consists of the time-series model, Kalman filter model, parametric regression model, and so on, while the other consists of the nonparametric regression model, wavelet transform model, multi-dimensional fractal model, spectral basis analysis model, state space reconstruction model, and compound model with neural network (Sun *et al*. 2004) (Ma *et al*. 2015). The models used widely are the history average model, time-series model, neural network model, and nonparametric regression model.

DOI: 10.1201/9781003217367-4

TABLE 4.1

Main Properties of the Collected Freeway Toll Data

S. No.	Name	Description
1.	V_{ID}	Vehicle identifier
2.	S_N	Source name
3.	D_N	Destination name
4.	T_{In}	T-In time in of the vehicle entry
5.	T_{Out}	T-out time out of the vehicle
6.	V_h	Number of vehicles crossed per hour

4.3 Dataset Collection

To evaluate traffic flow, toll data was gathered from two different toll plazas on a freeway network in Bangalore city for two weeks in January. The gathered data can be examined to forecast the traffic structure and avoid traffic congestion during peak hours and particularly on holidays. The properties of the freeway toll data are given in Table 4.1.

This work used a traffic flow dataset for traffic flow prediction, congestion avoidance, and fuel usage reduction. This dataset contains traffic flow details between Chennai, Vellore, Bangalore, and Nelamangala. It has ten attributes:

1) Vehicle_Id

2) Source

3) Destination

4) Route

5) Distance

6) Average_Speed

7) Time_to_Reach_Destination

8) Entry_Time

9) Exit_Time

10) Vehicle_Type

SAMPLE DATASET

VehicleId, Source, Destination, Route, Distance, Speed, TimeToReach, EntryTime, ExitTime, VehicleType

TN 58 BH 6268, Bangalore, Vellore, Bangalore-Ambur-Vellore, 214, 22.7, 9.4, 26-01-2020 06:15 AM, 26-01-2020 06:36 AM, HPMV

TN 32 RN 4848, Nelamangala, Vellore, Nelamangala-Makali-Bangalore-Ambur-Vellore, 246, 22.7, 10.8, 26-01-2020 06:25 AM, 26-01-2020 06:42 AM, LMV

TN 33 SU 3507, Vellore, Bangalore, Vellore-Ambur-Bangalore, 214, 22.7, 9.4, 26-01-2020 06:30 AM, 26-01-2020 06:51 AM, LMV

TN 99 TZ 0176, Bangalore, Chennai, Bangalore-Ambur-Vellore-Kanchipuram-Chennai, 361, 22.7, 15.9, 26-01-2020 06:34 AM, 26-01-2020 06:51 AM, HPMV

TN 17 ZM 4261, Nelamangala, Bangalore, Nelamangala-Makali-Bangalore, 32, 22.7, 1.4, 26-01-2020 07:03 AM, 26-01-2020 07:14 AM, LMV

TN 65 OL 1677, Nelamangala, Bangalore, Nelamangala-Makali-Bangalore, 32, 22.7, 1.4, 26-01-2020 07:09 AM, 26-01-2020 07:25 AM, HPMV

TN 85 KK 6316, Nelamangala, Vellore, Nelamangala-Makali-Bangalore-Ambur-Vellore, 246, 22.7, 10.8, 26-01-2020 07:13 AM, 26-01-2020 07:46 AM, HPMV

TN 48 TH 0715, Bangalore, Chennai, Bangalore-Ambur-Vellore-Kanchipuram-Chennai, 361, 22.7, 15.9, 26-01-2020 07:25 AM, 26-01-2020 07:59 AM, HMV

TN 40 LJ 8787, Nelamangala, Chennai, Nelamangala-Makali-Bangalore-Ambur-Vellore-Kanchipuram-Chennai, 393, 22.7, 17.3, 26-01-2020 07:47 AM, 26-01-2020 08:03 AM, HPMV

TN 21 GN 4761, Vellore, Bangalore, Vellore-Ambur-Bangalore, 214, 22.7, 9.4, 26-01-2020 07:47 AM, 26-01-2020 08:19 AM, LMV

TN 53 MU 8138, Chennai, Nelamangala, Chennai-Kanchipuram-Vellore-Ambur-Bangalore-Makali-Nelamangala, 393, 22.7, 17.3, 26-01-2020 08:00 AM, 26-01-2020 08:18 AM, LMV

4.4 Traffic Flow Analysis

An intelligent transportation system (ITS) creates numerous solutions using Big Data analytics to enhance traffic scenario problems. Numerous ITS applications are launched to improve a range of aspects of the Indian traffic system like intersection control, vehicle classification, historical traffic data, incident detection, and monitoring. Traffic congestion is a very familiar problem in several metropolitan cities in India. Most cities require a smart traffic management system to forecast congestion and to help avoid accidents before they happen.

In India, due to heterogeneous traffic conditions, road safety and congestion have become major issues for both vehicle users and pedestrians. Most cities are experiencing a major growth in population and face many challenges as they expand and grow at an increasing rate. Traffic is one of the most challenging issues in all developing cities. Table 4.2 shows the measures taken by some highly regarded cities in controlling traffic.

TABLE 4.2

Traffic Measures

S. No.	Name of the City	Measure
1.	Stockholm	Electronic road pricing
2.	Barcelona	Urban Lab – dynamic traffic forecasting
3.	London	Electronic journey planner
4.	Hong Kong	Public light bus
5.	Copenhagen	Integrative public transport model
6.	Hangzhou	Public cycling system
7.	United Kingdom	Active traffic management approach

Modern traffic management systems are widely needed in India for managing traffic conditions across various developing cities. Mumbai introduced a modern traffic management system. A real-time tuning traffic flow system was adopted whereby traffic intensity was detected by the installed video cameras and the data was downloaded to a computer. This helped in making real-time traffic signal adjustments, helping travelers feel better and creating a well-organized traffic flow system across the city. It was also feasible to track and deal with black spots from the control center. From the control center, accidents or damaged vehicles or huge traffic jams can also be monitored and handled extremely quickly.

Big Data analytics and ITS jointly provide solutions for traffic situations under abnormal conditions. This work proposes a prediction method which can be adopted by most Indian cities. This prediction method uses the information collected from one of the toll roads connecting Bangalore. A toll road is a public or private roadway for which a fee is charged for passage. It is a form of road pricing typically implemented to help recoup the cost of road construction and maintenance, which amounts to a form of taxation. The work considers Bangalore, one of the most important IT development cities in India, in terms of the prediction of traffic flow.

Bengaluru, also known as Bangalore, is the capital of the South Indian state of Karnataka. This is the third most populated city in India, with more than 8 million people. Also called the Garden City, it is well known for its pleasant climate throughout the year and attracts many travelers. Bengaluru is the fastest developing major metropolitan city in India. With the sudden growth of IT sectors, this city has become very populated and congested and faces various issues in terms of traffic management systems. It is also home to many of India's educational and research institutions. Many people also often visit the city for various purposes. Managing traffic and avoiding congestion during peak hours is a major issue to be resolved. Especially during weekends and holidays, this city receives a huge number of vehicles, and managing traffic on those days is complicated. ITS applications provide smart solutions for traffic issues using data analytics and machine learning algorithms. Predicting short-term traffic flow will assist in managing the traffic system and improving traffic issues. Our proposed short-term traffic flow prediction method based on structure and pattern will improve the traffic system, which will also emphasize environmental issues and rerouting and will mean savings in both fuel consumption and time.

The various highway roads connecting Bangalore are shown in Figure 4.1 and the toll route path from which the toll data information was gathered is shown in Figure 4.2. Traffic congestion can be avoided by predicting the number of vehicles entering the city and finding the traffic structure pattern between the current station and upstream station. As six-wheelers and four-wheelers are much more common in Bangalore, it will be better if we predict congestion that happens because of these vehicles. To reduce congestion, four-wheelers and two-wheelers can be rerouted to save time and money. With this, fuel efficiency can also be achieved. The information from the toll was collected by manual observation of parameters at two toll plazas. The first toll plaza serves the Chennai–Bangalore National Highways, and second toll plaza serves the road connecting Tirupathi and Bangalore. The traffic between the current section and the upstream station (entering into the city) can be predicted to manage traffic efficiently.

The traffic flow analysis over the course of one week is shown in Figure 4.3. Making use of the massive amounts of toll data and data from sensors and cameras installed across the city at particular points of interest, we can identify the pattern of vehicle flow. The time of entry and exit of the vehicles moving from a particular region to another region and the total amount of time taken for transit between them, including overheads like traffic and

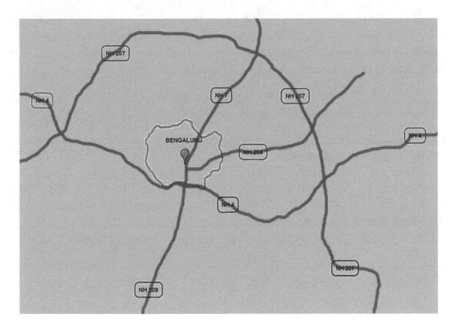

FIGURE 4.1
Highways connecting Bengaluru.

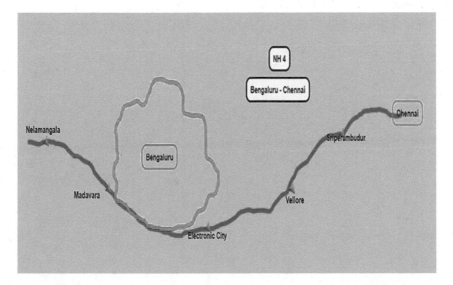

FIGURE 4.2
NH44-Highway route (sample).

other domestic problems, is to be calculated. Buses and other heavy vehicles are the main reason for traffic congestion. With these vehicular data, traffic congestion can be predicted and light vehicles can be asked to divert their route. The entry/exit of vehicles in a certain area and the traffic flow at a certain time interval can be found. The time period granularity is set at 20 minutes. The flow path of a vehicle can be represented as follows:

$$V_{Traj} = \left\{ \left(T_{V-in}, T_{v-out} \right) \right\} (i \geq 1) \tag{4.1}$$

where V_{Traj} means that a trajectory of a vehicle is through a consecutive road section in a city. $T_{V\text{-}in}$ means the entry time of the vehicle into the road section (i) entering into the city and $T_{v\text{-}out}$ means the exit time. It can cluster the set of vehicles that have passed. The structure of traffic flow at current time interval SV_R can be expressed as a vector

$$SV_{Ri} =< V_{Gi_1}, V_{Gi_2}, \ldots, V_{Gi_N} > \qquad (4.2)$$

Where SV_{Ri} represents the structure of a section of different vehicle types. V_{Gi_1} means the count of vehicles on the current road section at the current time interval. The sum of V_{Gi_1} is the traffic flow in this current section. To find out the traffic flow on a certain road section, we use an undersized set of components V_{Gi_1}.

If the vehicles are grouped mainly under three categories like LMV (light motor vehicles), HMV (heavy motor vehicles) and HPMV (heavy passenger motor vehicles), then the above traffic flow equation can be written as:

$$SV_{R1} =< V_{G1_1}, V_{G1_2}, \cdots, V_{G1_N} > \qquad (4.3)$$

where i represents the flow of LMV

$$SV_{R2} =< V_{G2_1}, V_{G2_2}, \ldots, V_{G2_N} > \qquad (4.4)$$

where i represents the flow of HMV

$$SV_{R3} =< V_{G3_1}, V_{G3_2}, \ldots, V_{G3_N} > \qquad (4.5)$$

where i represents the flow of HPMV

To compute the total number of vehicles in a particular road section at the current time interval,

$$V_{G1_1} + V_{G2_1} = V_{TC1}$$

$$V_{G1_2} + V_{G2_2} = V_{TC2}$$

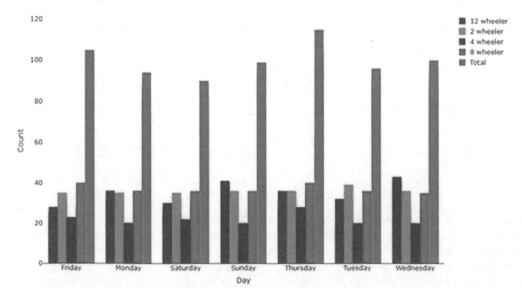

FIGURE 4.3
Traffic analysis.

Similarly,

$$V_{G1_N} + V_{G2_N} = V_{TCN} \tag{4.5}$$

Where $V_{TCk}(k \geq 1)$ represents the total number of vehicles of different types in a particular road section at the current time interval. Therefore

$$SV_R =< V_{TC1} + V_{TC2} + \ldots + V_{TCN} \tag{4.6}$$

The traffic on a particular road at a time interval of 20 minutes can be found using V_{TC1} which represents the traffic flow in the given time interval; V_{TC2} is the traffic flow on that particular road section in the next time interval.

4.5 Short-Term Traffic Flow Prediction

In order to forecast the traffic flow structure pattern between the stations, this work required data about the vehicles' source and destination and factual traffic information. The accuracy of the prediction method is most significant in irregular traffic states and particularly during peak hours. The prediction of the traffic flow structure pattern will improve the prediction system's accuracy. Prediction methodologies may not prevent congestion entirely, but can be helpful in congestion avoidance. An intelligent transportation system (ITS) supports various ways of improving traffic efficiency in many smart cities. From a holistic perspective, ITS exploitation is a key to maximize traffic efficiently and improving the congestion scenario. For example, ITS services have helped the Republic of Korea to increase the average speed of traffic by between 15 percent and 20 percent.

Providing real-time traffic information to travelers on the road is an efficient way to improve ITS. This will help to avoid traffic jams and also in managing vehicle speed wisely. With reduced traffic congestion and improved traffic efficiency, most public transportation services can be more reliable and punctual. This will also help in reducing traffic accidents and rash driving. Emergency vehicles like ambulances can be alerted before their arrival so that an alternate path can be taken to avoid congestion and thus save lives. This advance pre-empts accidents and reduces congestion.

4.5.1 Locally Weighted Learning (LWL)

Locally weighted learning (LWL) is a lazy learning method in which generalization beyond the training data is delayed until a query is made to the system. LWL is a set of function approximation techniques, in which a prediction is made by using an approximated local model around the current point of interest. This learning model deploys both linear and nonlinear models to fit the neighbor points and then applies those values to predict the values of the query points. LWL can also be used to include currently acquired data in the historical database to assist with learning. This algorithm can be used to achieve a high level of prediction accuracy (Atkeson *et al.* 1997),. This algorithm is lazy behavior and is based on an abundant training set. In some cases, unfortunately, this is too poor to support the learning process due to insufficient historical data and new queries. The regular traditional LWL would not be able to be used in abnormal traffic states, and certain strategies can be introduced to assist regression (Han *et al.* 2010).

The LWL algorithm can be effectively used in cases where historical data is abundantly available and there are no new queries. In the traffic prediction system, historical data is abundant, making LWL algorithms most suitable for traffic prediction involving both upstream and downstream traffics. This method can also be employed in scenarios involving undisciplined traffic. With this learning algorithm, the traffic structure pattern of the road section can be determined, and the spatiotemporal relationship between the traffic flow on the current section and the upstream section will be utilized.

4.5.2 Traffic Flow Structure Pattern Based Prediction Method

The main idea is to enhance LWL with the traffic flow stability structure pattern and to use the upstream station's entry flow to correct the forecast of the section traffic flow. The early concern is to direct LWL to choose inherent periodicity and feature space. This is due to the section flows' greater inherent periodicity; in particular, high-flow sections might have their volumes at prior hours recognized as features. The structure pattern of the current section flow is composed of less than four major components. To be clear, a small number of upstream stations have an influence on the current section. The entry flow from these upstream stations can be preferred as the feature of LWL. The variables used in the prediction methodology are described in Table 4.3.

In general, a standard regression model like $b = f(a) + \epsilon$ is assumed with a continuous function $f(a)$ and noise ϵ. The basic cost function of LWL is defined as

$$LW = \frac{1}{2}\sum_{i=1}^{n} w_i(a_q)(b_i - a_i\beta_b)^2 \tag{4.7}$$

TABLE 4.3

Variables Used in Prediction Methodology

Name	Description
TF_{ts}	Traffic flow of the target section
TF_{up}	Upstream station entrance flow
b_i	Data point
b_i	Traffic flow of target section corresponding to Xi
TD	Labeled training data
a_q	Query point, prediction
$d(a_i, \hat{b}_q = \hat{b}_q + S_r\beta_r)$	Relevance of training points
C_s	Components in flow structure
C_r	Input rate
C(t)	Correction function
V(t)	Prediction value
K(d)	Gaussian Kernel

With the components,

1) Labeled training data $TD = \{(a_i, b_i) - i = 1, 2, \ldots n\}$ where each data point a_i belongs to a corresponding output value b_i.

2) P.o.I. (point of interest or query point) a_q which is the position where we want a prediction $\hat{b}_q$.

3) Weight (w_i) describes the relevance of the corresponding training set for the current prediction.

4) Regression coefficient β_b is needed for prediction.

Algorithm 4.1 explains the traffic flow–based prediction method.

Algorithm 4.1 – Prediction Method Based on Traffic Flow
```
Step 1: Data collection in the given time granularity
Step 2: Compute SV_R1, SV_R2, SV_R3
Step 3: Compute the total number of vehicles in the current point of interest
        3.1 Calculate for each V_T
Step 4: Sequence of the queries (a_q = a_q - S_rP_r^n)
Step 5: Trace the vehicle trajectory and find the flow path - V_Traj
Step 6: Output - prediction vector (b̂_q)
Step 7: Process
            7.1 Initialization
                a) Select the structure pattern of the target section
                b) Decide upstream station based on the flow structure
                c) Compute the transfer time (Δt) and input rate (C_r) of
                    each upstream station
Step 8: Regression
            a) For each Query (a_q)
Calculate d (a_i, a_q) for each history points (a_i, b_i)
                b) Choose nearby neighboring points and arrange them in an order
                    according to their distance
                c) Obtain each points value based on Gaussian Kernel K(d)
                d) Compute V(t) and C(t)
                e) Prediction Vector (b̂_q), where b̂_q = α × V(t) + β × C(t). Initially α
                    and β values will be equal to 1
```

Sum the newly obtained points into the historical database of the pattern.

Algorithm 4.2 explains locally weighted projection regression (LWPR) prediction using nonlinear function approximation.

Algorithm 4.2 – Locally Weighted Projection Regression (LWPR) Prediction Algorithm – Nonlinear Function Approximation
```
Step 1: Input each query point a_q

Step 2: Initialize the values a_q = a_q - a_0 and b̂ = β_0
Step 3: Prediction
            For i = 1: R do
            S_r = u_r^T a_q  - Latent variable

            b̂_q = b̂_q + S_r β_r  - Update prediction
```

$$a_q = a_q - S_r P_r^n \text{ - Reduce input space}$$
End

4.6 Experiment Results and Discussion

This section analyzed the traffic flow structure pattern by considering the traffic flow in a week in January 2017. On abnormal days like republic day and Sundays, there were more HPMV vehicles traveling towards the city in addition to the frequent light motor vehicles and heavy motor vehicles that were running on those days. This leads to traffic congestion on the road which connects Chennai, Vellore, Bangalore, and Nelamangala. Predicting traffic on these days will help avoid traffic congestion. Light vehicles can be informed that they should take alternate routes to save time and improve fuel efficiency. Table 4.4 shows LMV vs. HMV vs. HPMV counts for all points of interest.

Figure 4.4 shows LMV vs. HMV vs. HPMV counts for all points of interest. This figure concludes that during peak hours (07.00 AM–10.00 AM and 05.00 PM–07.00 PM), congestion level is high. Therefore, each location suffers from heavy traffic in peak hours. Table 4.5 shows LMV vs. HMV vs. HPMV counts for Chennai.

TABLE 4.4

LMV vs. HMV vs. HPMV Counts for All Points of Interest

Time (in hours)	Vehicle Count (in hundreds)		
	LMV	HMV	HPMV
12.00 AM	6	6	4
1.00 AM	8	6	4
2.00 AM	2	4	7
3.00 AM	4	7	6
4.00 AM	6	4	6
5.00 AM	5	6	2
6.00 AM	7	4	3
7.00 AM	13	22	12
8.00 AM	38	41	37
9.00 AM	36	41	47
10.00 AM	28	41	21
11.00 AM	3	4	7
12.00 PM	7	2	8
1.00 PM	5	7	10
2.00 PM	3	7	6
3.00 PM	6	6	2
4.00 PM	7	4	3
5.00 PM	54	44	46
6.00 PM	41	66	44
7.00 PM	49	46	54
8.00 PM	6	8	5
9.00 PM	4	3	6
10.00 PM	7	9	4
11.00 PM	5	8	10

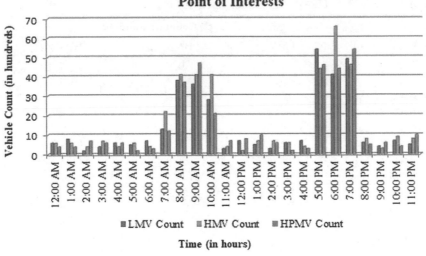

FIGURE 4.4
LMV vs. HMV vs. HPMV counts for all points of interest.

Figure 4.5 shows LMV vs. HMV vs. HPMV counts for Chennai. This figure concludes that during peak hours (07.00 AM–10.00 AM and 05.00 PM–07.00 PM), the congestion level becomes high in Chennai city. Therefore, Chennai city suffers from heavy traffic during peak hours. Table 4.6 shows LMV vs. HMV vs. HPMV counts for Vellore.

Figure 4.6 shows LMV vs. HMV vs. HPMV counts for Vellore. This figure concludes that during peak hours (07.00 AM–10.00 AM and 05.00 PM–07.00 PM), the congestion level b--+ecomes high in Vellore city. Therefore, Vellore city suffers from heavy traffic in peak hours. Table 4.7 shows LMV vs. HMV vs. HPMV counts for Bangalore.

Figure 4.7 shows LMV vs. HMV vs. HPMV counts for Bangalore. This figure concludes that during peak hours (06.00 AM–10.00 AM and 05.00 PM–08.00 PM), congestion level becomes high in Bangalore city. Therefore, Bangalore city suffers from heavy traffic in peak hours. Table 4.8 shows LMV vs. HMV vs. HPMV counts for Nelamangala.

Figure 4.8 shows LMV vs. HMV vs. HPMV counts for Nelamangala. This figure concludes that during peak hours (07.00 AM–10.00 AM and 05.00 PM–07.00 PM), the congestion level becomes high in Nelamangala city. Therefore, Nelamangala city suffers from heavy traffic during peak hours.

The minimum and maximum traffic levels during the period in question were shown in Figure 4.9. The first week's data were used for the prediction, while the following 7 days' was for prediction to test the model's performance.

Root mean square error (RMSE) was used to estimate the accuracy of the prediction, defined as

$$RMSE(b,b') = \sqrt{\frac{\sum_{n=1}((b(n)-b'(n))^2}{N}} \qquad (4.8)$$

TABLE 4.5

LMV vs. HMV vs. HPMV Counts for Chennai

Time (in hours)	Vehicle Count (in hundreds)		
	LMV	HMV	HPMV
12.00 AM	0	0	1
1.00 AM	2	2	2
2.00 AM	0	1	0
3.00 AM	0	2	0
4.00 AM	1	2	1
5.00 AM	2	0	1
6.00 AM	0	2	1
7.00 AM	4	8	1
8.00 AM	11	12	9
9.00 AM	5	13	13
10.00 AM	5	7	2
11.00 AM	0	1	1
12.00 PM	3	0	1
1.00 PM	0	1	3
2.00 PM	0	1	0
3.00 PM	3	3	0
4.00 PM	2	1	0
5.00 PM	14	20	8
6.00 PM	13	18	12
7.00 PM	13	12	16
8.00 PM	0	1	0
9.00 PM	1	0	0
10.00 PM	3	1	0
11.00 PM	3	4	3

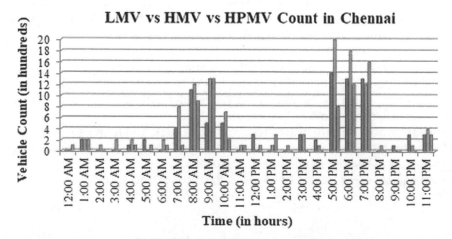

FIGURE 4.5
LMV vs. HMV vs. HPMV counts for Chennai.

TABLE 4.6

LMV vs. HMV vs. HPMV Counts for Vellore

Time (in hours)	Vehicle Count (in hundreds)		
	LMV	HMV	HPMV
12.00 AM	1	2	1
1.00 AM	2	2	2
2.00 AM	0	0	3
3.00 AM	3	2	5
4.00 AM	3	1	0
5.00 AM	1	0	1
6.00 AM	1	0	0
7.00 AM	2	6	3
8.00 AM	10	9	9
9.00 AM	7	5	11
10.00 AM	8	14	4
11.00 AM	2	0	1
12.00 PM	0	2	0
1.00 PM	2	2	1
2.00 PM	0	1	1
3.00 PM	0	1	1
4.00 PM	0	1	1
5.00 PM	15	7	14
6.00 PM	5	14	4
7.00 PM	14	13	13
8.00 PM	3	3	1
9.00 PM	3	1	3
10.00 PM	2	4	3
11.00 PM	0	2	1

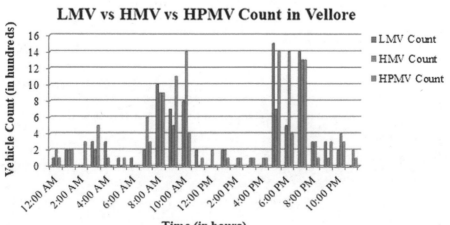

FIGURE 4.6

LMV vs. HMV vs. HPMV counts for Vellore.

TABLE 4.7

LMV vs. HMV vs. HPMV Counts for Bangalore

Time (in hours)	Vehicle Count (in hundreds)		
	LMV	HMV	HPMV
12.00 AM	3	0	1
1.00 AM	3	1	0
2.00 AM	1	2	1
3.00 AM	1	2	1
4.00 AM	2	1	2
5.00 AM	2	2	0
6.00 AM	3	1	2
7.00 AM	5	5	2
8.00 AM	8	11	6
9.00 AM	14	9	12
10.00 AM	6	10	8
11.00 AM	1	0	2
12.00 PM	2	0	4
1.00 PM	2	3	4
2.00 PM	1	2	2
3.00 PM	2	1	1
4.00 PM	1	1	0
5.00 PM	13	9	12
6.00 PM	12	17	18
7.00 PM	8	10	10
8.00 PM	0	3	2
9.00 PM	0	1	1
10.00 PM	1	0	0
11.00 PM	1	1	4

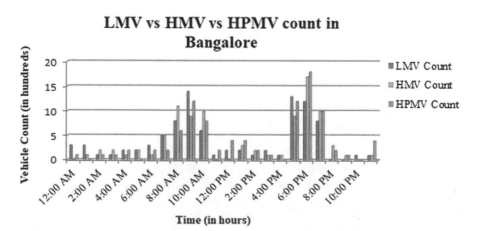

FIGURE 4.7
LMV vs. HMV vs. HPMV counts for Bangalore.

TABLE 4.8

LMV vs. HMV vs. HPMV Counts for Nelamangala

Time (in hours)	Vehicle Count (in hundreds)		
	LMV	HMV	HPMV
12.00 AM	2	4	1
1.00 AM	1	1	0
2.00 AM	1	1	3
3.00 AM	0	1	0
4.00 AM	0	0	3
5.00 AM	0	4	0
6.00 AM	3	1	0
7.00 AM	2	3	6
8.00 AM	9	9	13
9.00 AM	10	14	11
10.00 AM	9	10	7
11.00 AM	0	3	3
12.00 PM	2	0	3
1.00 PM	1	1	2
2.00 PM	2	3	3
3.00 PM	1	1	0
4.00 PM	4	1	2
5.00 PM	12	8	12
6.00 PM	11	17	10
7.00 PM	14	11	15
8.00 PM	3	1	2
9.00 PM	0	1	2
10.00 PM	1	4	1
11.00 PM	1	1	2

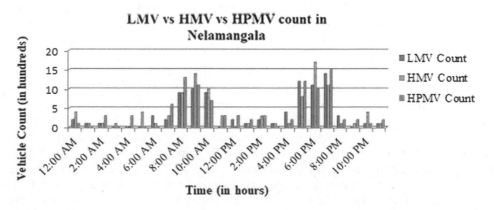

FIGURE 4.8

LMV vs. HMV vs. HPMV counts for Nelamangala.

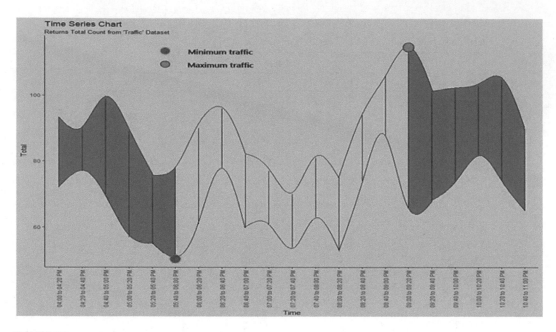

FIGURE 4.9
Maximum and minimum traffic in the duration period.

TABLE 4.9

RMSE of Experiments

RMSE	Traditional LWL	STTPM
Day 4	35.60158	17.05670
Day 7	42.90654	20.04503

Where b is the actual quantity and *b'* is the corresponding prediction while N is the total number of prediction values. The model with a smaller RMSE has better accuracy. The experiment results are given in Table 4.9.

Table 4.9 concludes that the proposed method is better than the traditional LWL method on the considered day. On other days and holidays, the proposed method provides better results accurately and efficiently. This system is better able to deal with a sudden increase in traffic flow and can support finding the maximum traffic in the given duration.

The maximum and minimum traffic are shown in Figure 4.10. Traffic was found to be maximum during weekends and government holidays; this can be used to predict the traffic during abnormal states. To verify the stability of the structure pattern, this work uses the coefficient of variation (CV) as a stability index (Jin *et al.* 2004). The coefficient of variation is the percentage variation in mean and standard deviation being considered as the total variation in the mean. The series of data for which the coefficient of variation is large indicates that the group is more variable and it is less stable or less uniform. If a coefficient of variation is small, it indicates that the group is less variable and it is more stable or more uniform.

Figure 4.11 shows how the distribution of data is displayed based on five categories: minimum, first quartile, median, third quartile, and maximum. IQR is the interquartile range.

(Figure 4.12) shows a comparison between the proposed approach and the regular LWL approach. The line in red is the trained model prediction line on which comparison is

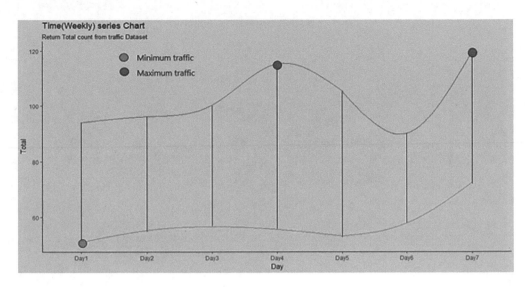

FIGURE 4.10
Maximum and minimum traffic.

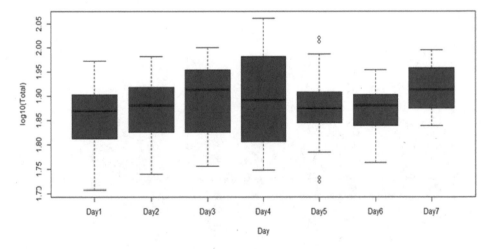

FIGURE 4.11
Distribution of data especially on holidays.

made. The yellow line is the regular approach, and the green line is the proposed approach. The line that is closer to the red line can be considered as a superior approach. In this, we can observe that at most places or data points, the green line is smoother than the yellow line and closer to the red line. According to the data collected and used, STTPM is the finest prediction model. This shows the proposed system results are 30 percent better than regular approaches.

The proposed approach is compared with various existing system approaches and the comparison is shown in Figure 4.13. The efficiency of the proposed scheme is shown in the figure and tables, and the results prove the efficiency of the proposed system. The proposed short-term traffic prediction based on traffic structure pattern is superior and more efficient than other approaches.

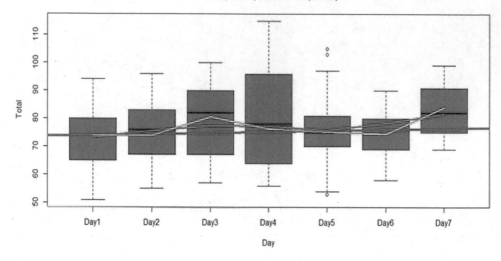

FIGURE 4.12
Comparisons of LWL vs. STTPM.

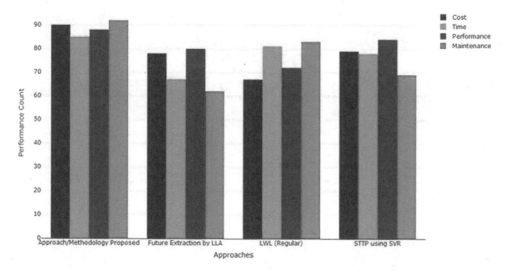

FIGURE 4.13
Comparison of approaches.

4.7 Summary

This chapter proposed an efficient short-term traffic flow prediction methodology based on traffic flow structure pattern and regression methods. The chapter analyzed traffic flow congestion on the two most frequently traveled roads. The traffic flow at the subsequent time point can be predicted by using entrance flow information. Initially, this work collected data to predict traffic flow, and then the traffic occurring at the next stations was determined. With the pattern information and LWL, this work predicts the traffic flow over the course of a week. The results show that prediction based on a structure pattern is an effective approach for predicting traffic flow in metropolitan cities. This would be more useful for predicting abnormal traffic conditions in India.

5

An Efficient Intelligent Traffic Light Control and Deviation System

5.1 Introduction

Currently, the capability of roads and transportation systems has not evolved to such an extent that they can cope efficiently with the increasing number of vehicles and growth in population. Due to this, traffic jams and road congestion have increased. TomTom R reported that in 2014, commuters spent on average 66 more hours stuck in traffic than they did in 2013, and a visit which might take 60 minutes in noncongested traffic will take 57 minutes longer during rush hour (Alsrehin *et al.* 2019). Since expansion of the prevailing road network is currently restricted, it is essential to develop technologies to ensure the road infrastructure is well organized, allowing smooth traffic flow.

Traffic congestion issues have some other indirect overlooked issues such as noise, pollution, and increased traveling times. INRIX reported that economic loss in the U.S. due to traffic congestion was estimated at \$121 billion in 2011 and is expected to increase up to \$199 billion in 2020 (Schrank *et al.* 2015). With all these concerns in mind, it was essential to think of a solution to overcome these concerns and manage traffic. Traffic forecasting and management is a popular issue in big and smart cities, and it has become a critical concern.

City municipalities, governments, companies, and researchers have proposed many solutions to solve the traffic jam problem. Some of these solutions are the use of adaptive traffic signals, vehicle-to-infrastructure smart corridors, autonomous vehicle technology, real-time traffic feedback, tracking pedestrian traffic, car sharing, and multi-modal solutions. Most of these solutions are based on the concepts of the Internet of Things (IoT), wireless sensor networks (WSN), and data analytics (DA) approaches. Other partial solutions that have been suggested include 1) the construction of new roads, bridges, tunnels, flyovers, and bypass roads; 2) and creating ring roads and performing road rehabilitation.

Traffic congestion refers to a situation in which an increased number of vehicles on a given stretch of roadway at a specific time leads to slower speeds and longer trip times, and it is a serious challenge in the area of traffic management and transportation planning (Raj *et al.* 2016). It cannot be completely eliminated, but it can be remediated to some extent. Informing road users in advance about the road status will help to minimize the chance of traffic congestion occurring and allow road users to make better decisions during their journey. This information includes quantifiable measures for traffic congestion, which may be represented by estimating some traffic parameters like time period and traffic density. Measuring these parameters from the field is very difficult (Raj *et al.* 2016).

For travelers, traffic congestion means lots of time spent on their journey, missed opportunities, and frustration. For employers, it means losses in terms of worker productivity and trade opportunities, delivery delays, and increased costs. Reducing traffic congestion will allow people to travel safely, reduce number of accidents, reduce fuel consumption, help in controlling air pollution, reduce waiting times, allow for the smooth motion of cars along transportation routes, and help in providing the required data for future road planning and analysis.

There are different causes of traffic jams, like insufficient capacity, unrestrained demand, large red-light delays, and obstacles on the road like accidents, random vehicle stops, double parking, road work, and road narrowing. Traffic generates huge amounts of data that are collected from different types of devices, such as intelligent cameras and sensors. So, there is no issue in collecting these data; the challenging issue is how to store, handle, process, analyze, and manage the increased amounts of traffic data to make effective use of it. The abovementioned approaches mainly focus on analyzing a huge amount of traffic data to extract certain aspects of this data, including but not limited to traffic speed, traffic volume, vehicle arrival rate, and average waiting time.

To control traffic and to avoid congestion in urban undisciplined traffic, an efficient framework is proposed in this chapter. This will resolve the issues in any metropolitan city. Parameters used in vehicle measurement are vehicle count, vehicle categorization, vehicle speed, and traffic arrival probability. A traffic deviation system is employed to divert the route path of the vehicles intelligently, which results in the avoidance of traffic congestion. The main contributions of this chapter are 1) An intelligent light traffic control system to control heavy traffic flow in metropolitan cities; 2) an intelligent deviation system to divert the traffic to avoid congestion; and 3) valuable traffic parameters for a traffic control management system.

5.2 An Efficient Intelligent Traffic Light Control and Deviation System

This section describes an efficient traffic light control and traffic deviation system which also consists of vehicle detection and count, vehicle categorization, and determination of the speed and length of the vehicle. Several traffic issues can be resolved efficiently. An intelligent agent system (Iscaro & Nakamiti 2013) was proposed using a supervisor agent system. This approach is not efficient since it requires double agents to observe the entire process. A controller and supervisor are the two agents used.

In our multi-agent system approach, for activities such as collecting and processing data, an agent is assigned, namely supervisor agent and controller agent. The vehicle count and categorization is done by the data collector agent. The assessment of vehicle length and speed and the possibility of determining the comparative vehicle weight is done by the data processor agent. Finally, the light control method is employed, which depends on the data processed. This will help to reduce traffic congestion but this may not eliminate traffic congestion problems completely, so we have introduced a deviation approach to make the system function better. The proposed system architecture is depicted in Figure 5.1.

5.2.1 Elements of the Proposed Framework

The constituent elements of the proposed model and functions are explained here.

5.2.1.1 Sensors

A wireless magnetic sensor is chosen as traffic sensor since it is flexible, less complex to install, lower cost and reliable inductive loop detector system. Four sensors are used (SN0,

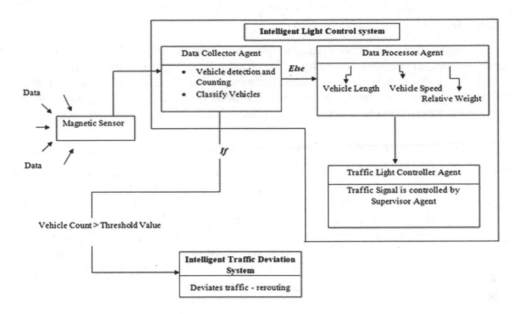

FIGURE 5.1
Architecture of an efficient intelligent traffic light control and deviation system.

SN1, SN2, SN3). All the sensors are disseminated suitably in relation to the traffic. One sensor was intended for traffic lights. The traffic administration decides the distance between the sensors' locations. To make the deviation signal system receive the signal, another sensor is used.

5.2.1.2 Data Collector Agent

This agent task is to examine the data composed through the sensors; they are vehicle count and vehicle categorization. In the proposed approach, data collector is a component and it is a part. This acts as first representative in the multi agent system approach.

5.2.1.3 Data Processor Agent

This agent is next in the traffic system. Its role is to determine vehicle length and velocity and the relative quantity of traffic. In the proposed system, the data processor agent acts as a part of the system. The traffic data will be manipulated by the data processor and the input will be sent to the intelligent traffic light control system. Both the agents are independent.

5.2.1.4 Intelligent Traffic Light Controller

Various traffic and traffic security issues, such as traffic hijacking, rerouting, and traffic jams, will be handled by a secret supervisor agent. This will decrease traffic issues but is not guaranteed to solve them completely. Hence a traffic congestion prediction system is needed for an intelligent transportation system. This system has a threshold value depending on the traffic area, and if the value exists, then an alert signal will be sent to the deviation system.

5.2.1.5 Intelligent Traffic Deviation System

If a congestion situation is predicted, the deviation system provides a signal to deviate vehicles arriving in the congested path. Whenever this is required, this system will play the role actively. Another sensor is placed to divert the traveling vehicles; this will be performed by the deviation system. Once an alert is made by the intelligent deviation system, vehicles are not permitted to use the same route.

5.2.2 Vehicle Detection and Counting

Magnetic sensors are used to detect vehicle counting and also for communication between the sensor plates, since this sensor has improved measurement capability. Counting incoming vehicles on the arrival route is a random process. To determine the number of incoming vehicles in a time period T ($t1$, $t2$, ...), Poisson distribution can be used. Poisson distribution can be applied to get vehicle arrival information in a random system. In finding the number of vehicles arriving and modeling the random process at a given time period, Poisson distribution is used conventionally. To calculate the probability of a definite amount of vehicles arriving during a certain length of time, then t would be the length of time and n would be the number of vehicles. The flow rate would be given as λ. λ and t should be computed using the same time units.

Probability of v vehicles in a period of time can be represented in equation form as:

$$P(v) = e^{-\lambda}\left(\frac{\lambda^k}{k!}\right) \tag{5.1}$$

where
v = the vehicles, which may take values from 0, 1, 2, ...
$P(v)$ = probability of the event v
λ = average number of vehicles
e = 2.71828 (Euler's number)
$v! = v \times (v-1) \times (v-2) \times ... \times 2 \times 1$ is the factorial of v

This computation will be made for each and every time period (T). We assume the flow rate (λ) = 300 vehicles/hour = 300/60 = 5 vehicles/minute. Probabilities of the vehicles observed are specified in Table 5.1. In this, N represents the count of vehicles passed in an hour.

5.2.3 Vehicle Categorization

In categorizing the traffic management applications, vehicle categorization is more important. Road planning, maintenance, and organization; model design and development; traffic signal control system design, and so on are among the different categories included in the traffic management system classification. Vehicle classification can be used to assess the size of the vehicle on either side. While categorizing individual vehicles, exact measurements are needed. In this approach, vehicles are divided into nine groups based on the highway classification.

5.2.4 Compute Vehicle Length Depending on Speed

In traffic flow conditions, vehicle length is the most important parameter. Congestion problems can also be predicted on this basis. It is the most important research issue in an

TABLE 5.1

Probability of Vehicle Arrival Rate

N	$P(\nu)$	$F(\nu) = P(\nu) \times N$
0	0.0190	1.9086
1	0.0832	4.8934
2	0.1546	8.9816
3	0.1973	11.736
4	0.1973	11.736
5	0.1564	9.387
0.1039	6.912	7
0.0596	3.547	8
0.0301	1.873	9
0.0141	0.785	10
0.0053	0.318	

intelligent transportation system (ITS). Vehicle length was measured only for the duration of the red series and green series in a similar period in Cheung *et al.* (2005). This approach was not efficient in calculating the length of the vehicle. So, in this chapter, we propose computing vehicle length along with the velocity rate. Since the arrival rates of vehicles are random, velocity cannot be determined randomly since it increases costs. This chapter proposes computing the vehicle length, which depends on the vehicle speed rate, by using a magnetic sensor. Some sensors that are suitable for road traffic systems are discussed. Piezo sensors are used to collect, count, and classify; pneumatic road sensors are applied to record vehicles; to detect vehicle movement, microwave detectors are used; proximity sensors are applied in detecting when the vehicle gets close to an object; and road tube counters are used to collect data on vehicle volume.

Here,

$$t = \Delta T_{End} - \Delta T_{Begin} \tag{5.2}$$

Velocity can be determined by

$$\upsilon_{avg=} {}^{\Delta D_{End} - \Delta D_{Begin}} \big/ {}_{t}$$

υ_{avg} = average velocity

ΔD_{End} = destination final

ΔD_{Begin} = destination begin

ΔT_{End} = time to reach the end

ΔT_{Begin} = begin time from the initial stage

t = time period

The vehicle length can be computed by

$$L = T \times \upsilon \tag{5.3}$$

where L = length, T = interval time period, and υ = velocity.

Once the vehicle length is computed, then it is easy to determine the speed rate of the vehicle. The speed can be computed by S=N/L, where S=Speed, N=No. of vehicles, and L=length.

5.2.5 Light Control System and Measurement of Vehicle

The whole weight is computed by means of adding up the values of all sensors located on two sides of the road and the relative mass of the vehicles. If the vehicles are moving with the same speed and have the same length, this approach (Salama *et al.* 2010) will work. Since traffic flow is a random process, this may occur randomly. So to compute, we use various traffic parameters.

The traffic information collector (TLC) agent collects the traffic information, and the data will be stored. The light controller agent controls the traffic indication using the traffic information which was transferred to the undisclosed supervisor agent. Then the data processor will process the data and provide the input to the TLC controller agent. Finally, the effective smart light control system can be achieved by computing whole average weight, vehicle length, and speed by adding up the sensor values and the relative mass of the vehicles' probability on each road as

$$T_{AW}\left(RT_k\right)_{k=1\to4} = \sum_{j=0}^{3} SN_j + P_k + S_k + L_k \tag{5.4}$$

where,

$T_{AW}\left(RT_k\right)$ = total average weight

SN_j = sensors placed at roadside

P_k = relative weight probability

S_k = speed of vehicle

L_k = length of vehicle

5.2.6 Traffic Deviation System

When the intelligent traffic light control mechanism works well, several traffic issues can be reduced, but they may not be completely eliminated. An intelligent traffic deviation system can also be used. This system diverts traffic onto various other alternative routes to avoid traffic blockage problems before they occur. In avoiding traffic issues, this system will have an important role in preventing traffic congestion. This can be applied in various geographical areas. Hence this model will be efficient in outlying parts of the city or in high traffic issue areas to avoid traffic congestion. With this approach, traffic congestion can be prevented in advance. The work flow of the traffic deviation system is shown in Figure 5.2.

5.3 Results and Discussion

An intelligent traffic light control and deviation system will prevent congestion problems and assist in route deviation. This proposed scheme will be appropriate for a range of geographical areas. Therefore this model can be used in outlying areas of the city or in

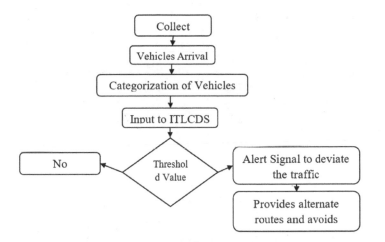

FIGURE 5.2
Work flow of the traffic deviation system.

FIGURE 5.3
Sample model route map.

areas with high levels of traffic to avoid traffic congestion before vehicles get to the area in question.

In Figure 5.3, the outer border region of Chennai is considered as a sample model and the notations used are explained in Table 5.2. In the figure, the route towards Chennai is represented in violet, and the deviation route is represented in red. The model is a simple case of vehicle deviation. Therefore the proposed intelligent traffic congestion avoidance and deviation system can be used in particular areas which have deviating route ability. Instead of constructing new roads to reduce traffic congestion, vehicles can be deviated to avoid congestion and this also leads to several benefits for travelers like savings in fuel consumption, cost, and time and also in maintaining a green environment.

In Figure 5.4, if any vehicle is traveling from A to B, it requires a time $t1$ (x is said to be the distance from A to B). If there happens to be any traffic congestion on the traveling route, then the traveling time of the vehicle will be increased; say $t1 + \mu$ is the time taken to reach the destination B (μ will represent the delayed time). When the vehicles are diverted, then

TABLE 5.2

Notations

S. No.	Symbol	Meaning
1.	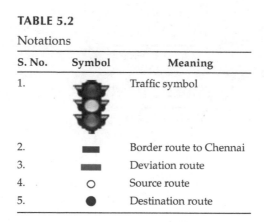	Traffic symbol
2.	▬	Border route to Chennai
3.	▬	Deviation route
4.	○	Source route
5.	●	Destination route

the vehicle takes *t*2 time to get from A to B (a deviating signal is used to divert the vehicles). This deviated alternate route may be slightly longer than the regular route, but with this the speed of the vehicle can be increased and the vehicle will be free from traffic congestion. This will help in reaching the destination quickly and also results in a relaxed trip.

Figure 5.5 shows an intelligent traffic deviation system. First, it finds all congested routes between Bangalore and Chennai. It then extracts all available routes between Bangalore and Chennai. Then, it computes the congestion probability for a specific time interval. If the congestion probability is above the threshold value, this system considers that route has heavy traffic; otherwise it is normal. So, it chooses a less congested route for a diversion route.

5.3.1 Conversion of Map to Graph

This work used a fascinating discovery made by Euler, which makes possible a graph using the six color theorem. The considered graphs are first mathematically segmented into a number of vertices and edges.

Iscaro and Nakamiti (2013) note that "Euler has proved in a different manner, where the number of vertices minus the number of edges plus the number of faces of a polyhedron is always equal to two", and that "Any planar graph has Euler characteristic equal to 2".

$$X = V - E + F$$

Where V is the vertex of the map, E is the edges of the map, and F is the faces of the map.

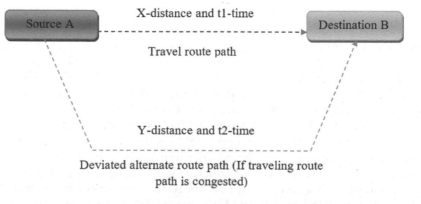

FIGURE 5.4

Traffic system assumption.

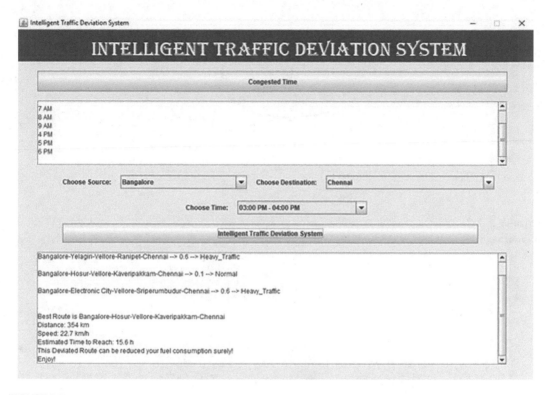

FIGURE 5.5
Intelligent traffic deviation system.

If a graph has a single vertex, then the value of X is equal to 2 ($V - E + F = 1 - 0 + 1$). So, if additional vertices are joined to each edge for each vertex, the answer is always 2.

Figure 5.6 represents a map of Chennai that has been converted to a graph with the help of the six color theorem. Six color nodes are fixed as six places; each node is related, with the root node being Chennai. The diagram provides the various route paths going towards Chennai city. Before the beginning of the city boundary, the vehicle population is determined, and then the vehicles are diverted via various different routes to enter the city.

5.3.2 Validation

The proposed system was assessed in terms of a range of issues such as the quantity of time spent by a vehicle in the traffic queue, fuel consumption, and time expenditure. Using the proposed deviation system, the time spent in the traffic queue can be reduced. Fuel and time wastage can be avoided. Figure 5.7 elucidates the assessment of the performance of this system with available related systems. The methodology is compared in terms of performance and cost. The approach by Zhu and Jin (2011) makes use of single loop detector and this method uses 15th percentile vehicle passage time over the detector that will be used in speed estimation. Chiu and Chand (1993) make use of a single magnetic sensor, reducing the traffic cost and as a result are 63 percent better than the other technique. Taghvaeeyan and Rajamani (2013) use a sensing system and achieved 95 percent, and Coifman (2001) computes individual vehicle lengths and achieved 85 percent. Based on

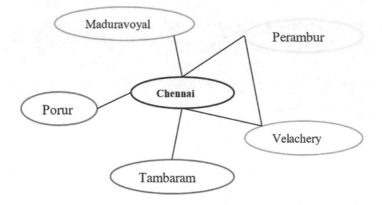

FIGURE 5.6
Graph from map.

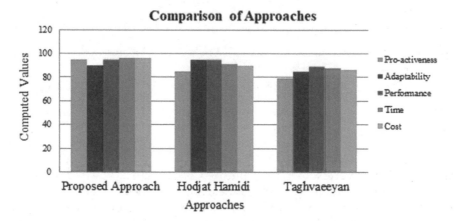

FIGURE 5.7
Comparison of approaches.

the previous works, only one parameter was addressed by all of them, but the framework offered here incorporates all the parameters and offers solutions for various traffic problems. Netlogo was used to test the proposed system by considering the real Chennai traffic flow dataset (Salama *et al.* 2010). A multi-agent monitoring model is proposed (Hamidi & Kamankesh 2018), which monitors the traffic conditions and guides drivers in case of an emergency. The proposed approach is an agent-based approach. The proposed system comprises two solutions for traffic problems: a traffic light control system and a traffic deviation system. So, if any traffic congestion is predicted, traffic issues can be resolved using the traffic deviation system. According to Liu *et al.* 2007), the test statistic used by the proposition is given by a Z-test calculation:

$$\overline{Z} = \frac{\overline{d}}{Sd/\sqrt{n}}$$

The performance evaluation of the proposed system with the various related systems is shown in Figure 5.7. Proactiveness, adaptability, performa nce, time, and cost are the various key factors considered for the comparison between various approaches. The magnetic wireless sensor has some constraints in terms of signal processing, like noisy situations (Chen *et al.* 2001). To determine the vehicle count in a given interval of time, Poisson distribution can be used and a Nagel–Schreckenberg model can be used to validate it; this is a theoretical model for freeway traffic. This model is suitable only for traffic congestion that is increasing without any external influences. Most of the research has provided various algorithms for a particular aspect like vehicle length, vehicle classification, vehicle speed, etc., which are not sufficient for the traffic system. This chapter integrates various factors like vehicle length, vehicle speed, and vehicle classification to make the traffic system control the traffic more effectively and efficiently. A new traffic deviation approach is introduced to avoid traffic congestion completely.

Figure 5.8 illustrates the traffic density of the system prior to deviation and after deviation. Consequently, the values of average velocity of the vehicles are assumptions taken under the normal computation of the traffic flow. The values are computed in the same way as the above assumptions. This graph depicts that traffic density is reduced after deviating the vehicles. These graphs are drawn based on the analysis of the traffic system. Both the figures represent the traffic density; Figure 5.8 shows the density before adopting the traffic deviation method and the density after adapting the traffic deviation method. The curve in the figure proves the efficiency of the proposed system by showing that the traffic conditions are optimal.

Figure 5.9 shows traffic light controls in the cities of Chennai, Vellore, Bangalore, and Nelamangala from 08.00 AM. The data processor agent processes data based on vehicle length and speed. Then, the traffic light controller agent calculates the total average weight of the road. Then it controls traffic lights based on red, yellow, and green lights. This agent flashes red for less average weighted roads, yellow for medium average weighted roads, and green for high average weighted roads in a progressive manner.

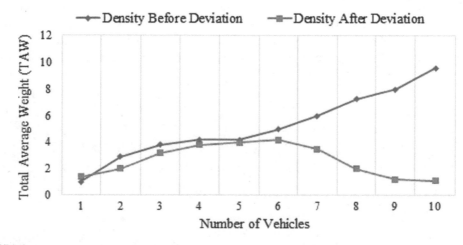

FIGURE 5.8
Traffic density before and after deviation.

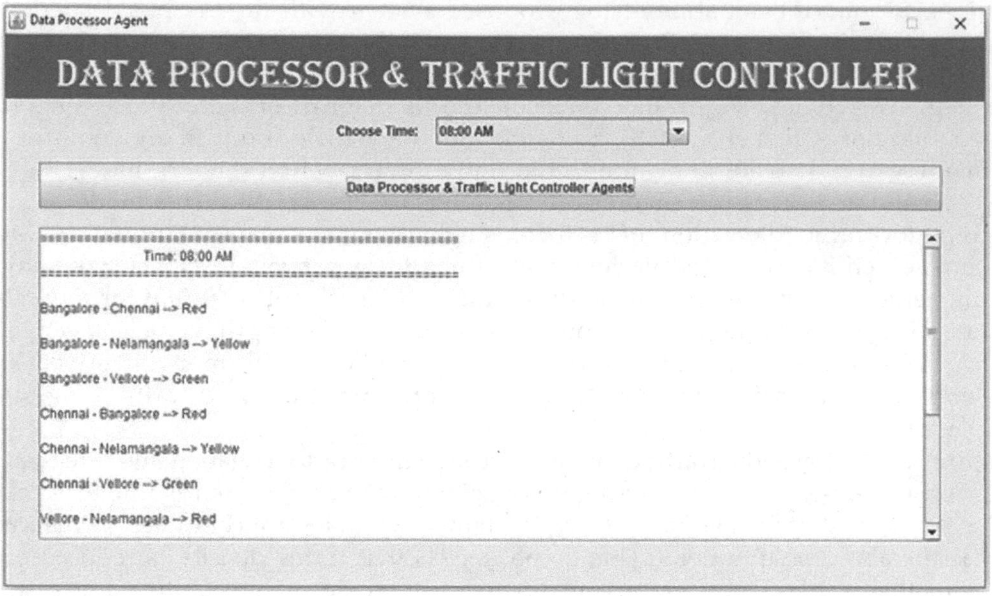

FIGURE 5.9
Traffic light controls.

5.4 Summary

In this chapter, an efficient intelligent traffic system is proposed to minimize the traffic congestion problem before it happens. This system will decrease the traffic queue size and provides an alternative route for vehicles to avoid traffic and to achieve a free flow of vehicles. An intelligent traffic light control system is deployed to prevent traffic congestion before it occurs and, based on an alert signal, the traffic will be diverted. This can help the travelers to have free-flowing traffic. Traffic jams could be avoided and the condition of the traffic flows in many metropolitan cities could be improved. Euler's approach used to convert maps to graphs was tested on a metropolitan city graph and the results were found to be satisfactory. Ultimately, the overall framework is statistically proven to be better than the related traffic congestion models.

6

IoT-Based Intelligent Transportation System (IoT-ITS)

6.1 Introduction

The Internet of Things (IoT) involves connecting physical objects to the Internet to build smart systems. The growing population in metropolitan areas in this modern age requires more smart services for transportation. Achieving smart and intelligent transportation involves the use of millions of devices connected to the IoT. An IoT-based intelligent transportation system (IoT-ITS) helps in automating railways, roadways, airways, and marine routes, enhancing customer experience in terms of the way goods are transported, tracked, and delivered.

6.2 Internet of Things

In the past two decades, the proliferation of new technology has made a huge impact on people's lifestyles. Emerging technologies have developed features that are tightly aligned with people's interests, like being compact, easier to use, feature-rich, connected to the Internet, fast, and smart. The availability of affordable sensors, together with the proliferation of Internet infrastructure, enables an interesting technology called the Internet of Things (IoT).

Figure 6.1 represents the Internet of Things. IoT resulted from context aware computing by Perera *et al.* (2013), which aims to allow people and things to be connected anytime and anywhere with anything/anyone. In other words, devices and applications have the ability to communicate with each other without or with less human influence. There is also significant interest and attention towards IoT from the industry. This interest has triggered the development of a myriad of sensors for different applications like location sensing, weather forecasting, biomedical applications, and many more. Many companies have developed a custom board targeting IoT applications.

Smart cities utilize multiple technologies to improve the performance of health, transportation, energy, education, and water services (Kyriazis & Varvarigou 2013), leading to higher levels of comfort among their citizens. This involves reducing costs and resource consumption in addition to more effectively and actively engaging with their citizens. One of the recent technologies that have a huge potential to enhance smart city services is Big Data analytics. As digitization (Gaur *et al.* 2015) has become an integral part of everyday life, data collection has resulted in the accumulation of huge amounts of data that can be used in various beneficial application domains. Smarter cities are based on smarter

DOI: 10.1201/9781003217367-6

FIGURE 6.1
Internet of Things.

infrastructure. There are many ways that IoT can help governments build smarter cities (Angelidou 2015). One method is through optimizing services related to transportation, such as traffic management, parking, and transit systems. There is no single consensus as to the definition of a smart city, but there is some agreement that a smart city is one in which information and communication technology (ICT) facilitates improved insight into and control over the various systems that affect the lives of residents.

Smart transportation, a key Internet of Things vertical application (Sta 2017), refers to the integrated application of modern technologies and management strategies in transportation systems. These technologies aim to provide innovative services relating to different modes of transport and traffic management and enable users to be better informed and make safer and "smarter" use of transport networks.

Intelligent IoT-enabled transportation systems improve capacity, enhance travel experiences, and make moving anything safer, more efficient, and more secure. Local police, emergency services, and other government services can use these sensor networks in tandem with smart traffic management to gain citywide visibility so as to help alleviate congestion and rapidly respond to incidents. IoT-based intelligent transportation systems are designed to support the smart city vision, which aims at employing advanced and powerful communication technologies for the administration of the city and the citizens.

Cities, as we all know, face complex challenges, and for smart cities, the outdated traditional methods of planning transportation, environmental contamination, finance management, and security observations are not adequate. The developing framework for the smart city requires a sound infrastructure and the adoption of the latest current technology. Urbanization and globalization mean that modern cities are under pressure to improve the quality of life of their citizens.

The expansion of Big Data and the evolution of IoT technologies have played an important role in the feasibility of smart city initiatives. Big Data offer the potential for cities to obtain valuable insights from a large amount of data collected through various sources, and the IoT allows the integration of sensors, radio-frequency identification, and Bluetooth in the real-world environment using highly networked services. The combination of the IoT and Big Data is an unexplored research area that has brought new and interesting challenges for achieving the goal of future smart cities.

These new challenges focus primarily on problems related to businesses and technologies that enable cities to actualize the vision, principles, and requirements of the applications of smart cities by realizing the main characteristics of the smart environment. In this paper, state-of-the-art communication technologies and smart-based applications are used within the context of smart cities. The potential for Big Data analytics to support smart cities is discussed by focusing on how Big Data can fundamentally change urban populations at different levels. Moreover, a future business model of Big Data for smart cities is proposed, and the business and technological research challenges are identified. This study can serve as a benchmark for researchers and industries for the future progress and development of smart cities in the context of Big Data.

Intelligent transportation systems are advanced applications that aim to provide innovative services relating to different modes of transport and traffic management and enable various users to be better informed and make safer, more coordinated, and smarter use of transport networks. Experfy deploys advanced analytics on a wide range of intelligent transport system technologies such as car navigation, traffic signal control systems, container management systems, variable message signs, automatic number plate recognition, and speed cameras. Experfy also provides analytics for advanced applications that integrate live data and feedback from a number of other sources, such as parking guidance and information systems, weather information, and bridge de-icing systems.

In 2010, the European Union defined intelligent transportation systems (ITS) as systems "in which information and communication technologies are applied in the field of road transport, including infrastructure, vehicles and users, and in traffic management and mobility management, as well as for interfaces with other modes of transport".

Smart transportation includes the use of several technologies, from basic management systems such as car navigation, traffic signal control systems, container management systems, automatic number plate recognition, or speed cameras to monitor applications, such as security CCTV systems, to more advanced applications that integrate live data and feedback from a number of other sources. ITS technologies (Khajenasiri *et al.* 2017) allow users to make better use of the transportation network and also pave the way for the development of smarter infrastructure to meet future demand. The evolution of intelligent transportation systems is providing a growing number of technology solutions for transportation managers as they seek to operate and maintain these systems more efficiently and improve performance.

According to the Intelligent Transportation Society of America, ITS technology makes it possible to:

- Use a navigation system to find the best route based on real-time conditions.
- Alert drivers of potentially hazardous situations in time to avoid crashes.
- Be guided to an empty parking space by a smart sign.
- Ride a bus that turns traffic lights green on approach.
- Detect and respond promptly to traffic incidents.
- Reroute traffic in response to road conditions or weather emergencies.

- Give travelers real-time traffic and weather reports.
- Allow drivers to manage their fuel consumption.
- Adjust speed limits and signal timing based on real-world conditions.
- Improve freight tracking, inspection, safety, and efficiency.
- Make public transportation more convenient and reliable.
- Monitor the structural integrity of bridges and other infrastructure.

An example of the benefits of the implementation of smart transportation technologies can be found in Austria, where the country's Autobahn and Highway Financial Stock Corporation (ASFiNAG) turned to Cisco's Connected Roadways solutions to bring the IoT to its roadside sensors (Kim, T-h *et al.* 2017). The result is a highway designed to monitor itself, send information to drivers, and predict traffic to ensure lanes stay clear of congestion.

By all accounts, IoT and Big Data represent a huge opportunity for cost savings and new revenue generation across a broad range of industries. Researchers provided a primer on IoT and described how IoT impacts the manufacturing industry (Kummitha & Crutzen 2017) in the first two briefs in the IoT series. This brief will highlight several examples of how IoT is being used to create smarter cities. In its most basic definition, the Internet of Things describes a system where items in the physical world, and sensors within or attached to these items, are connected to the Internet via wireless and wired network connections. The Internet of Things will connect inanimate objects as well as living things. IoT will connect everything from industrial equipment to everyday objects that range from medical devices to automobiles to utility meters.

6.3 Intelligent Transport System

An intelligent transportation system (ITS) plays a major role in contributing towards smart city development. In most developing countries like India, public transportation systems (bus) are the main source of travel for many commuters living in urban as well as rural areas. An intelligent transportation system (ITS) theme is to develop a prototype for ITS, which will be useful to track a vehicle through GPS, payment of tickets, and crowd analysis inside the bus through near field communication (NFC); finally, the atmosphere inside the bus can be measured with temperature and humidity sensors.

Figure 6.2 shows an intelligent transportation system. Within an IoT infrastructure, the data collected from sensors is sent through the Internet and processed by the monitoring system to make useful decisions and send it to the display system (as per application requirements). ITS groups the entire architecture into three systems: the sensor system, the monitoring system, and the display system. The sensor system utilizes GPS, NFC, and temperature and humidity sensors, which are always connected with the Internet via a Global System for Mobile Communications (GSM) network to track the location, commuter, and atmosphere inside the bus.

The monitoring system is intended not only to extract the raw data from the sensor database and convert it into meaningful information but also to trigger events within the bus as well as provide information to the bus driver. The display system is used to show the context data regarding bus and travel information to all the commuters at the bus stop.

FIGURE 6.2
An intelligent transportation system.

6.4 IoT-Based Intelligent Transport System

Objects that appear to intelligent transportation sector development offers remarkable transportation to provide a wider development space, and thus modern opportunities to introduce new horizons for the development of intelligent transportation, requiring "Internet of Things." The new generation of intelligent transportation developments provides important technical support for the realization of real-time, efficient, accurate, safe, energy-saving intelligent transport objectives and provides technical support for Internet of Things technology, and networking technology will improve intelligent urban traffic.

The growing population in metropolitan areas in this modern age requires more smart transportation services. Achieving smart and intelligent transportation requires the use of millions of devices equipped with IoT technology (Sheng-nan *et al.* 2015). For example, the Toronto Intelligent Transportation Systems Centre and Testbed developed a system known as MARLIN-ATSC (Multi-agent Reinforcement Learning for Integrated Network of Adaptive Traffic Signal Controllers) (Sherly & Somasundareswari 2015) to improve traffic flow through the use of smart signals that process traffic information locally. Tests of the system on 60 downtown Toronto intersections at rush hour showed a reduction in delays of up to 40 percent. The test also showed that the system cut travel times by as much as 26 percent.

Singapore has adopted an intelligent transport strategy and set of systems. It has one of the least congested major cities, with an average car speed on main roads of 27 km/hr., compared to an average speed of 16 km/hr. in London and 11 km/hr. in Tokyo. The city uses an electronic road pricing system whereby the tolls vary according to traffic flows. It has an expressway monitoring and advisory system that alerts motorists to traffic accidents on major roads. It also has a GPS system installed on city taxis, which monitors and reports on traffic conditions around the city. Information from all of these systems is fed into the intelligent transport system's operations control center, which consolidates the data and provides real-time traffic information to the public. Figure 6.3 shows an IoT-based intelligent transportation system.

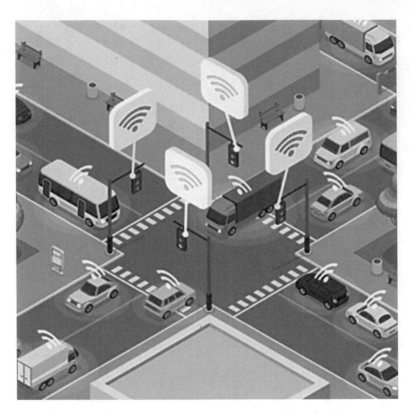

FIGURE 6.3
IoT-based intelligent transportation system.

6.5 S-ITS System Overview and Preliminaries

A smart intelligent transportation system (s-ITS) includes a range of components such as a central server, radio frequency identification (RFID) devices, sensors, lighting control units, and EBOX II. The central server plays a major role in providing resilience during any malfunctioning of the system. RFID helps in communicating data flow information between the cars and the EBOX II. This RFID device has tags, antennas to communicate information, and readers to decode the data. Figure 6.4 shows the proposed smart intelligent transport system.

6.5.1 Design Requirements of ITS System

- The RFID tag operates on a specified frequency. The ITS system to be built is required to have ultra-high frequency. This helps in achieving a good range and recognizes data within about 4–6 meters.
- The energy needed for the operation of the RFID device and lighting control unit is provided by extra chargers.

6.5.2 Design Goals

The system considers the following parameters in designing a new ITS system.

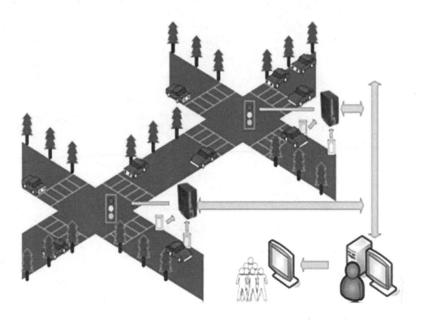

FIGURE 6.4
Proposed smart intelligent transport system.

6.5.2.1 Scalability

The s-ITS system designed must cater to the growing data world, namely Big Data. The information should be portable and the settings must be able to be remotely operated without any hindrance.

6.5.2.2 Reliability

As the smart transportation system is designed to operate without any manual intervention by humans, and it is of utmost importance that the system must be reliable. It should also be designed to handle any unexpected situations in an efficient way.

6.5.2.3 User-Friendliness

The user need not be aware of the entire implementation. Rather, the user needs to know the initialization in a single click and the admin must also be able to manage any mishaps that occur on the server side.

6.5.3 Experimental Design

The proposed system smart intelligent transport system involves the smart building of the intelligent transport system with the ability to tackle issues in real time. The intelligent system is built to address the following modules.

a) Vehicular location tracking
b) Intelligent vehicle parking system
c) Communication within a vehicular ad hoc network (VANET)
d) Vehicular Big Data mining

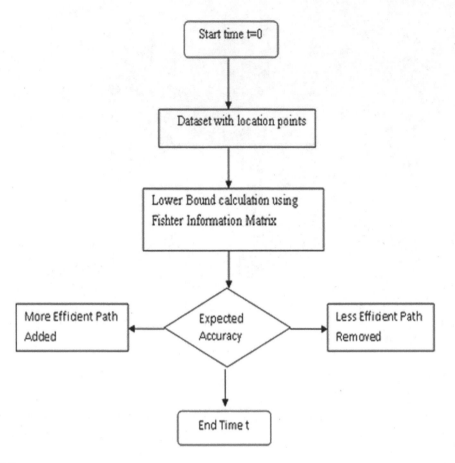

FIGURE 6.5
Flow of the s-ITS vehicle localization.

The proposed algorithm helps in selecting those paths that provide maximum accuracy. With the lower bound value accuracy value as the benchmark, the model is checked for its performance. So if the model achieves better targeted accuracy than that of the lower bound, then it implies there are enough paths which are efficient, and all other less accurate connection paths are discarded. If the lower bound is more than the expected accuracy rate, then it implies that there are not enough paths in the selected ones. Further, the necessary routes are added to the set for effective vehicle localization. Figure 6.5 shows an s-ITS vehicle localization flow diagram and the pseudocode shows path sensing–based vehicle location tracking.

```
Pseudocode for vehicle location tracking by path sensing
Inputs: C_i^1 represents the connections of a vehicle at time 1.
        N_i^{1-1} represents the connections composed by the proposed
        algorithm at time 1-1.
β (1 - 1) Represents the vehicle's position at time 1-1.
        D[K] is the location of the unit at the time K.
α is the expected accuracy.
Step 1: Z_i[k] = A β_i [1 | 1 - 1] which represents initial elements.
```

```
Step 2: N_i^1 = N_i^{1-1} C_i^1
Step 3: If | C_i^1 | > 5 then i = fisher (D[k], Z_i[k], σ_{ij2})
Step 4: Else I = 0.5 α^{-2} end if

Step 5: μ = √(Trace{I^{-1}}) - α

Step 6: If α < 20%α then
Step 7: N_i^1 = N_i^1 - M_i^1
Step 8: For I ∈ N_i^1 do
Step 9: Z = fisher(D[k], Z_i[k], σ_{ij2})
Step 10: [b] = Trace{ I^{-1}Z{I^{-1}}
Step 11: End for
Step 12: Else if α > 20%α then
Step 13: If N_i^1 C_i^1 - D^k = then
Step 14: N_i^1 = N_i^1 - M_i^1 else
Step 15: For I ∈N_i^1 C_i^1-D^kdo
Step 16: Z = fisher(D[k], Z_i[k], σ_{ij2})
Step 17: [b] = Trace{ I^{-1}Z{I^{-1}}
Step 18: End for
Step 19: I_{max} = {j ∈ N_i^1 [b] = {max{b}}}
Step 20: N_i^1 = N_i^1 + i_{max} end if
Step 21: Else
Step 22: N_i^1 = N_i^1
Step 23: End if
```

6.5.3.1 Vehicular Location Tracking

The vehicle localization algorithm predicts the location of the vehicle at time 1. This involves the storing of the predicted set and later measuring if the count of the predicted set is greater than 5. If so, then the Fisher value is calculated. If it is less than 5, then the Fisher value is not calculated and it is ensured that more new connections are added. Then, as per the flow, the lower bound accuracy calculated from the Fisher matrix is compared with the predicted value. If there is improvement in the predicted accuracy value, then extra connections could be removed. Thus, the proposed algorithm has the advantage of reducing the time period of the selection of paths for the vehicles as well as easy location estimation.

6.5.3.2 Intelligent Vehicle Parking System

Sensors play a major role in this module. They help in collecting information about the geographic location of the vehicle, availability of parking spaces, prior reservation details, position of the parking, details regarding the vehicle itself, and current traffic information. Thus Big Data plays a major role here as it involves the real-time application of the facility to provide an intelligent system for transportation.

Vehicle parking decisions are made by outcome factors like whether the space is occupied or free. If the space is free and available for parking, then it is marked as free. If there are vehicles in the location, then it is marked as occupied. The parking decision is based on the application of the outcome value which will be updated over a period of time through sensors. The decision is then updated in the server. The features are compared against the given threshold value for the final determination of the parking space. Figure 6.6 shows the s-ITS parking scheme.

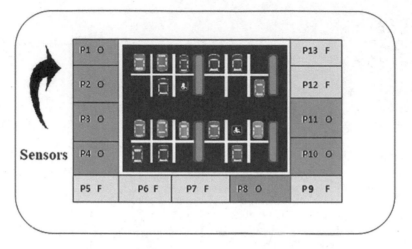

FIGURE 6.6
Parking scheme of s-ITS.

6.5.3.3 Communication within a VANET

With the help of the prior registration of the vehicle and its device, the sensors track the location of the vehicle and its status in the current traffic scenario. By using the sensor systems of IoT, the data is transferred and transmitted between the vehicles such that it helps in avoiding traffic and also ensures a safe journey.

6.5.3.4 Vehicular Big-Data Mining

The system built is made to inform users in advance about the traffic conditions and dangerous road situations; it also must be capable of handling unforeseen accidents and situations with data so that it could be provided in advance to vehicles for safe driving. It is important that the signals be communicated to the vehicles through the mining of the huge volume of previous similar data and also on the basis of the current traffic status.

6.5.4 Implementation

The implementation of the s-ITS involves ensuring that the proposed system achieves intelligent transportation through localization and by avoiding traffic using Big Data techniques.

In Figure 6.7, Chennai city is taken as an example, and the traffic levels on various roads are represented by different colors on the map. The various Big Data techniques and their application for ITS are depicted below.

6.5.4.1 Big Data Techniques in ITS

Multivariate analysis involves analyzing more than two variables at a time, thereby delivering some useful results in a shorter period of time. Univariate analysis is extended to hold more variables for analysis. In the case of linear regression, two variables are analyzed, whereas in a multivariate structure, more predictor variables are used.

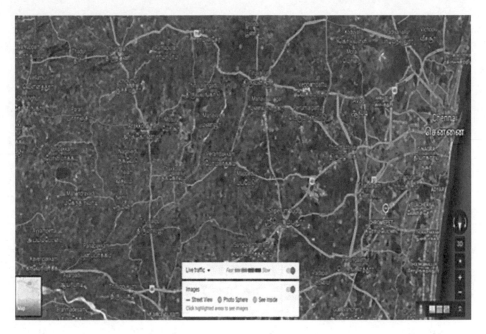

FIGURE 6.7
Map of Chennai for indicating traffic levels of the s-ITS.

6.5.4.2 Classification of Multivariate Techniques

The classification is based on the variable's ability to be segregated into dependent and interdependent forms. A dependent form is one in which a variable is declared as a dependent variable; this is to be predicted by other variables, which are independent variables. An interdependent form is one in which no variable is dependent or independent. The flow graph shows some multivariate techniques. Figure 6.8 shows the classification of multivariate techniques with relevance to s-ITS.

6.5.4.3 Multiple Regression Analysis

The method of multiple regression aims to predict changes in a dependent variable in response to changes in an independent variable. This technique is found to be of benefit when the problem to be addressed involves a single dependent variable related to two or more independent variables. This is achieved by the method of least squares.

$$\underset{(\text{metric})}{Y_1} = \underset{(\text{metric, nonmetric})}{X_1 + X_2 + X_3 + \ldots + X_n}$$

This multiple regression can be applied to ITS, wherein the time (dependent variable) at which the vehicle reaches the destination could be predicted by using the traffic on the route, the speed of the vehicle, etc. (independent variables). This makes the prediction simpler and it can be depicted in a metric and nonmetric form as in the equation.

6.5.4.4 Multiple Discriminant Analysis

This technique is suitable when the total population can be divided into several groups based on a dependent variable which has several relevant classes. The main objective is to

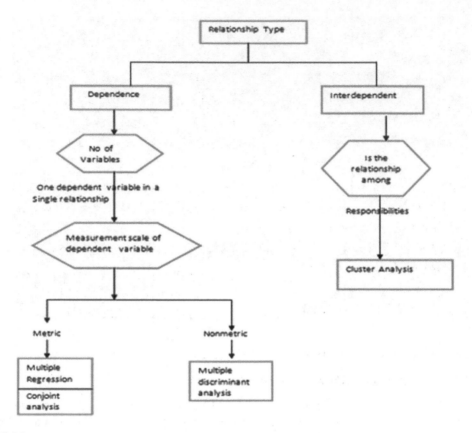

FIGURE 6.8
Classification of the multivariate techniques with relevance to the s-ITS.

understand the differences between the various groups and to predict the likeliness of an object to any of the groups based on the independent variable.

$$\mathbf{Y_1} \underset{\text{(nonmetric)}}{} = \underset{}{\mathbf{X_1} + \mathbf{X_2} + \mathbf{X_3} + \ldots + \mathbf{X_n}} \underset{\text{(metric)}}{}$$

Applying this technique to ITS, the best shortest routes that avoid traffic and help in reaching the destination earlier are obtained. This involves a usage of time factor and also a location-based route map.

6.5.4.5 Logistic Regression

The logistic regression model is a combination of multiple discriminant analysis and multiple regressions.

6.5.4.6 Conjoint Analysis

This analysis benefits both consumers and product researchers. When a product is designed with various attributes and parameters, customers are only concerned about certain parameters, while they ignore other parameters which do not interest them. Product researchers take keen note of all the attributes that will determine the marketing of that product. When relating this to s-ITS, the users of the vehicular system are concerned only about safe, collision-free travel. They want to know the parameters and techniques that will help them have safe journeys without congestion, whereas the system is intended to consider various aspects of vehicular movement and parameters that ensure uninterrupted travel with constant velocity. This is depicted as

$$\underset{\text{(nonmetric, metric)}}{Y_1} = \underset{}{X_1 + X_2 + X_3 + \ldots + \underset{\text{(nonmetric)}}{X_n}}$$

6.5.4.7 Cluster Analysis

Cluster analysis involves grouping the values into groups or clusters which determine the variations in the data elements. The process of clustering is done for a set of elements by finding the similarity of similar objects. Once the similarity is identified, the elements are grouped into respective clusters. The final step is to profile the final variables. In s-ITS, the parameters related to vehicle motion are grouped based on their relevance in determining the various factors that ensure vehicular motion, so that the transportation is made effective and collision-free.

6.6 Experiment Results and Discussions

The experiment results show that the proposed system outperforms existing ITS techniques in terms of throughput and packet delivery. It performs best in cases of delay and latency.

The above graph depicts the various parameters and their relevance with respect to different network schemes for communication of data in the form of packets. Figure 6.9 shows IoT based traffic congestion detection. This figure shows that during peak hours (04.00–06.00 PM and 07.00–09.00 AM) a lot of traffic congestion occurred. Furthermore, Figures 6.10 and 6.11 show the packet delivery ratio and packet delay comparison.

An IoT-based intelligent transportation system is shown in Figure 6.12 for the route from Bangalore to Chennai. Figure 6.12 predicts congestion details for all available paths and recommends an efficient route based on IoT devices.

Furthermore, Figure 6.13 shows vehicular location tracking. This figure shows that this IoT-ITS takes vehicle ID as input and provides vehicle tracking results.

Figure 6.14 shows IoT based intelligent vehicle parking system. This system guides vehicles to free slots. The proposed system shows the varied delay in different network scenarios. The recent version of the network, namely Enc 802.11 p, achieves a higher packet delivery ratio and lower delay.

The observations are made based on the basis of time and distance factors with respect to the metrics RMSE and MAPE. Figure 6.15(a) shows MAPE values vs. distance and Figure 6.15(b) RMSE values vs. distance. The proposed s-ITS is compared with existing techniques such as the fuzzy control rule and the fuzzy rule based on a genetic algorithm to determine their effectiveness. The observation is done for the Chennai region mainly during peak hours and in traffic-prone regions to find the best route. The proposed s-ITS helps in effective traffic monitoring as well as in easy parking as the vehicles are rerouted in case of traffic in a particular location.

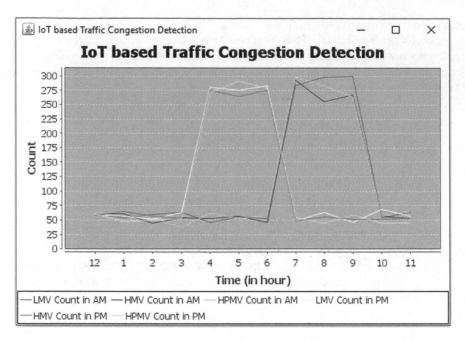

FIGURE 6.9
IoT-based traffic congestion detection.

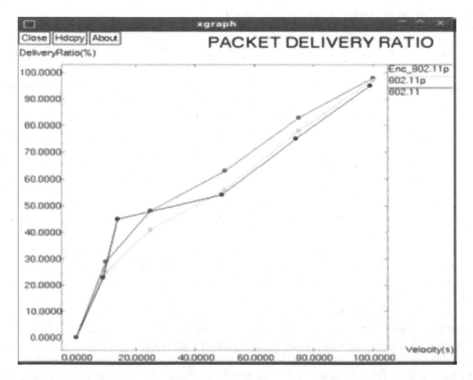

FIGURE 6.10
Packet delivery ratio comparison in various network environments.

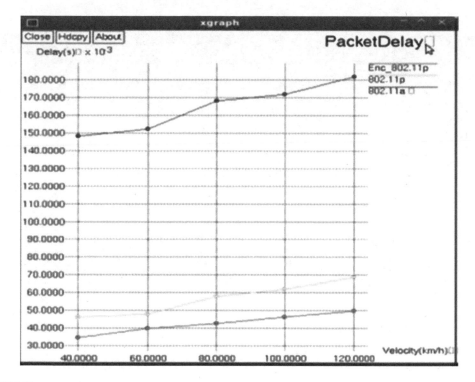

FIGURE 6.11
Comparison of packet delay in varied network environment.

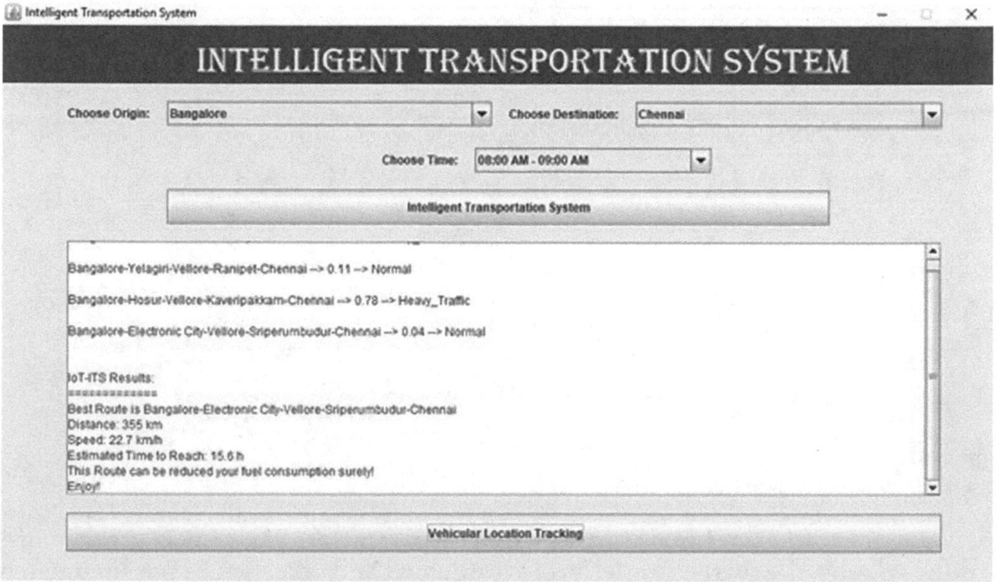

FIGURE 6.12
An IoT-based intelligent transportation system.

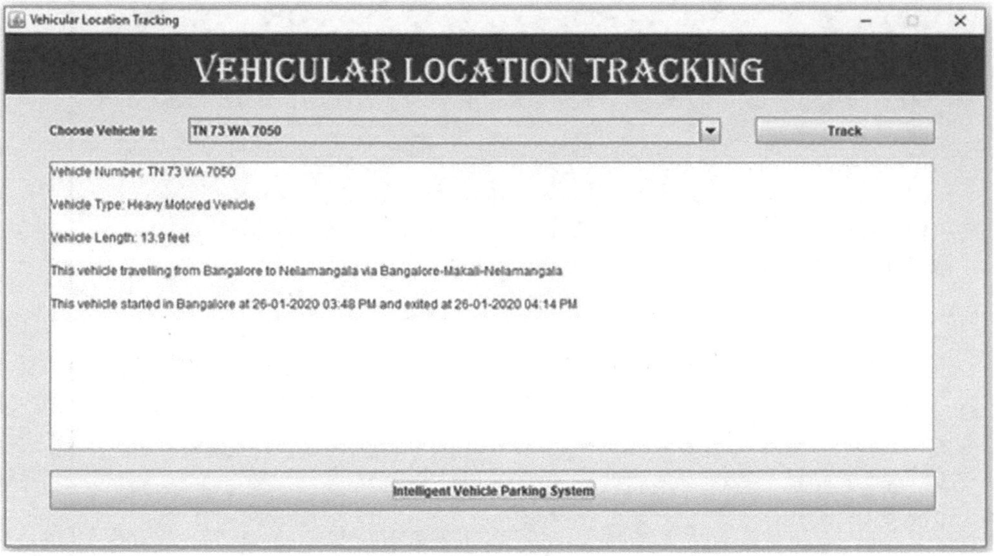

FIGURE 6.13
Vehicular location tracking.

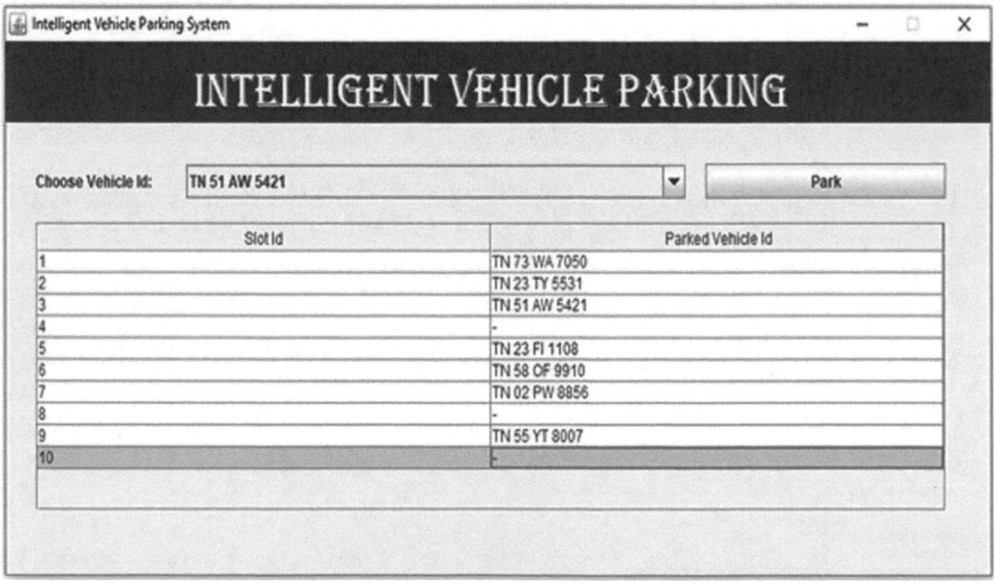

FIGURE 6.14
IoT based intelligent vehicle parking system.

Analyzing the traffic conditions further based on parameters like vehicle speed, density, and traffic volume, the current traffic level is estimated and vehicles are rerouted to reach their destination without further collision.

Figure 6.16 shows vehicle density comparison in various mechanisms. It shows that vehicle density is less with an increase in distance for the proposed system as the new system resolves traffic without much trouble. Also the vehicles are diverted to the alternate

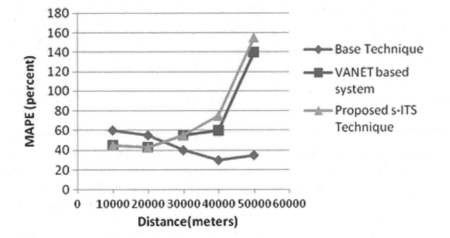

FIGURE 6.15 (A)
MAPE values vs. distance.

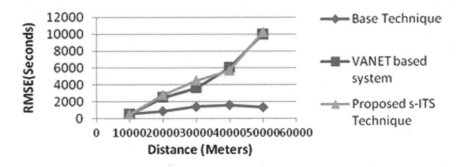

FIGURE 6.15 (B)
RMSE values vs. distance.

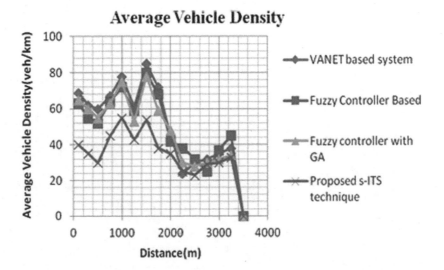

FIGURE 6.16
Comparison of vehicle density in various mechanisms.

path such that no congestion occurs. So the proposed system outperforms the other existing fuzzy-based and VANET-based systems by minimizing the vehicle count on a particular road without traffic.

6.7 Summary

This chapter has presented the overall architecture and the main components of an ITS based on an IoT infrastructure. It has also shown how our simple systems can be developed to realize an intelligent transportation system. The traffic data which is processed is then subjected to IoT and Big Data techniques and a framework, namely an s-ITS, is obtained. The proposed framework helps in location tracking of vehicles and smart parking and using Big Data technology to design an efficient transportation system. The system helps in monitoring vehicle motion, thereby determining the levels of traffic in a particular area. The proposed system has been evaluated for its performance in terms of packet delivery and network delay, and it was found that the proposed s-ITS system performs better than existing conventional systems. It is also exhibited through MAPE and RMSE values. Energy efficient mechanisms could be implemented in the ITS system and the system's efficiency could be made more promising in terms of dealing with the current road scenario.

7

Intelligent Traffic Light Control and Ambulance Control System

7.1 Introduction

The rapidly increasing vehicle population in India causes many issues in terms of transport management for emergency vehicles such as ambulances, the fire service, other emergency vehicles, etc., in the cities and towns of the country. Many patients are dead on arrival at hospital due to unpredicted traffic issues and there has been an inadequate response in terms of roadway improvement compared with other countries.

To minimize traffic problems typically faced by ambulances, an intelligent transport system is proposed. It is integrated with sensor information and communication technologies to achieve traffic efficiency, improve environmental quality, save energy, conserve time, and enhance safety and comfort, especially for ambulance drivers.

The proposed system has two modules, which communicate with and are controlled by sophisticated hardware components: an intelligent traffic light control system and an ambulance control system.

7.2 Intelligent Traffic Light Control System

Intelligent transportation systems involve the application of computer, electronic, and communication technologies and decision-making strategies in an integrated manner to provide traffic signaling information to emergency vehicles to increase the safety and efficiency of healthcare transportation systems. The main objective of the system is to use real-time information on the status of traffic to improve the transportation system's efficiency and productivity and to mitigate the adverse environmental impacts of the system.

The traditional traffic light control system has a significant disadvantage because the control time is fixed and cannot be adjusted, no matter the condition of the real-time traffic flow. Due to the set time control, the duration time of the green light, the red light, and the yellow light are fixed and constant at given road intersections. This weakness leads to a failure to solve the problem of traffic congestion smartly and intelligently. Therefore, it is necessary to design a smart signal traffic control system which can ensure the current duration time and also give priority to some lanes according to real-time traffic conditions. The system can ease traffic jams by raising the management level and improving the utilization rate of the road effectively. Figure 7.1 shows the intelligent traffic light control system.

Furthermore, Figure 7.2 shows a block diagram of the intelligent traffic light control system.

DOI: 10.1201/9781003217367-7

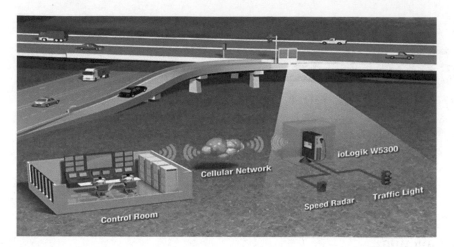

FIGURE 7.1
Intelligent traffic light control system.

7.3 Ambulance Control System

According to an experimental social survey conducted on how traffic reacts to ambulance sirens in India, many patients are dead on arrival at hospital due to unpredicted traffic situations and poor responses from people on the roads compared with other countries. The rapidly increasing vehicle population in India causes many issues in transport management for emergency vehicles such as ambulances, the fire service, and other emergency vehicles in the cities and towns of the country (Vanajakshi *et al*. 2010).

In this regard, this chapter proposes a solution to mitigate the challenges currently faced by emergency vehicle drivers using automatic intelligent signaling and route guidance. The main aim of this project is to resolve or at least minimize the traffic problems typically faced by emergency vehicles used in healthcare systems. The solution to this problem is achieved by integrating sensor information (direction of the ambulance), communication technologies (Xbee and radio frequency modules to transfer data from ambulance units and traffic control units), and analytics (decision making) so as to achieve traffic efficiency and ensure a speedy response from commuters. Further enhancement can also improve environmental quality, save energy, conserve time, and enhance safety and comfort, especially for emergency vehicle drivers (Fallah & Khandani 2016). Figure 7.3 shows an ambulance control system.

The following operational steps are carried out in the ambulance control system:

- Compass calibration for correct direction identification.
- Read compass data and send to universal asynchronous receiver transmitter (UART). UART is a computer hardware device for asynchronous serial communication in which the data format and transmission speeds are configurable.
- Place the ambulance module on the prototype, so that Z is pointing "up" and can measure the heading with x and y of the compass installed in the ambulance robot.
- Calculate heading when the magnetometer is level, then correct for signs of the axis.

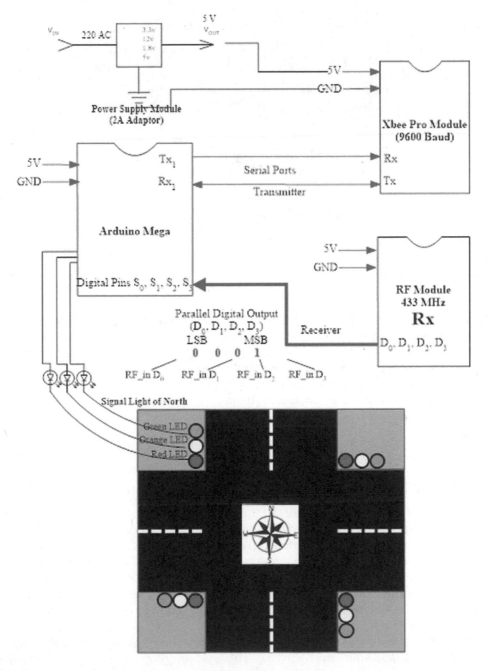

FIGURE 7.2
Block diagram of intelligent traffic light control system.

7.3.1 Traffic Coordination at Road Intersections

Even though intersections represent a small part of the entire road system, they account for a significant portion of traffic accidents. The approach proposed observes that the robustness of various sources of uncertainty must be considered, including model uncertainty, state (position, velocity, etc.) uncertainty due to imperfect sensors or due to vehicle-to-vehicle

FIGURE 7.3
Ambulance control system.

(V2V) and vehicle-to-infrastructure (V2I) communication (packet drops, random delays). An adaptive signal control method is proposed, comprised of a vehicle arrival estimation model and a signal optimization algorithm. Traffic flow modeling describes the application approach and procedures and demonstrates the accuracy and usefulness of macroscopic modeling tools for large-scale motorway networks. Furthermore, Figure 7.4 shows a block diagram of the ambulance control system.

7.4 Intelligent Traffic Light Control with an Ambulance Control System

Aiming to resolve or at least minimize the traffic problems typically faced by ambulances used in healthcare systems, the primary objective of the proposed intelligent transport system is to integrate sensor information and communication technologies to achieve traffic efficiency, improve environmental quality, save energy, conserve time, and enhance safety and comfort, especially for ambulance drivers.

Designed to operate traffic signals intelligently to enable emergency vehicles to move on without inconveniencing commuters, the intelligent traffic light control with the ambulance control system is shown in Figure 7.5.

A traffic light controller system with four traffic posts will control the traffic lights at 2-minute intervals (adjustable in software). This system is controlled by Arduino Mega and Arduino Uno controllers and has an Xbee Pro wireless module. The system contains an ambulance (robot module) with a siren tone on/off and blinking blue LED (light emitting diode) lights. This system is controlled by an Arduino Nano-Micro Controller Unit (MCU) and has an Xbee Pro wireless module along with direction compass sensors. As soon as the ambulance appears from any direction – North, South, East, or West (NSEW) – the traffic light system gives priority to it until it crosses the junction. Then, the traffic signaling system reverts to its original state.

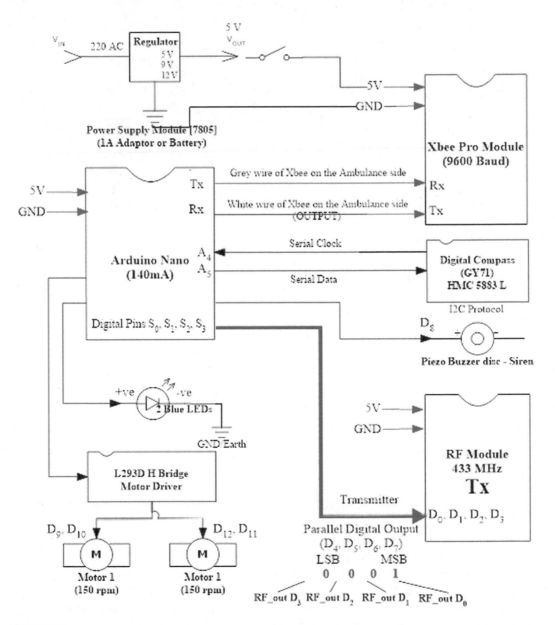

FIGURE 7.4
Block diagram of the ambulance control system.

7.4.1 Prototype Design Specification

To get a square model and have artwork that seems to be neater and more comfortable on top of the acrylic sheet, a prototype that resembles a traffic light intersection with a model of size 4' × 4' was built. This dimension would provide additional space to add features for future upgrades. Table 7.1 shows the components used.

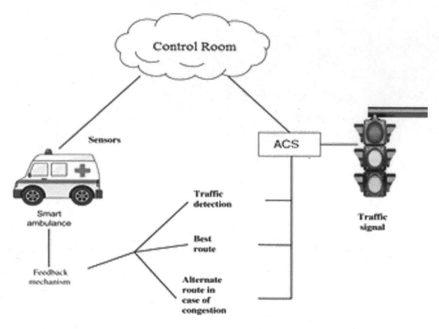

FIGURE 7.5
Intelligent traffic light control with ambulance control system.

7.4.2 Hardware Design and Connections

Hardware has been chosen in such a way that the system can be scaled for further enhancements to the project.

- Xbee Pro can communicate for >1km range and is useful for creating a mesh network.
- Arduino Mega is used in the traffic light control system, which has more resources such as Input/Output (I/O) ports and memory.
- Features such as traffic density estimation, a global system for mobile communication (GSM)/global positioning system (GPS) functionalities, countdown timers for each traffic post, pedestrian crossing, air quality monitoring, and productivity monitoring via IoT can be added in future.

7.4.3 Compass Sensor Library – ADAFRUIT

Adafruit Unified Sensor Driver: Many small embedded systems exist to collect data from sensors, analyze the data, and either take appropriate action or send that sensor data to another system for processing. One of the many challenges of embedded systems design is the fact that parts used today may be out of production tomorrow, or system requirements may change, and a different sensor may need to be chosen down the road. Creating new drivers is a relatively easy task, but integrating them into existing systems is both error-prone and time consuming since sensors rarely use the same units of measurement.

TABLE 7.1

Components Used

S. No.	Components	Quantity
1.	Arduino Mega module	2
2.	Arduino Nano module	3
3.	Multi-output power supply module	3
4.	XBee Pro Module – ZB Series 2SC – 63mW with Wire Antenna	3
5.	Xbee breakout modules	2
6.	Acrylic sheet – 8′ × 4′	1
7.	Robotic kit (chassis and metal rods)	2
8.	L293D motor drivers	2
9.	9V battery	3
10.	433Mhz encoder and decoder modules	3
11.	7805 regulators	3
12.	USB cable	3
13.	Piezo buzzers	2
14.	LED (5mm) with holder – red/yellow/green/blue LEDs	32
15.	Magnetometer sensor module	3
16.	12v/2A adaptor and connecting cables	3
17.	Push-button switches	4
18.	Connecting wires	5 mts
19.	PCB (2 × 4)	8
20.	Double-sided foam tape	2
21.	Foam sheet (black) – 8′ × 4′	1
22.	Acrylic paint	1
23.	Paint brush	1
24.	Nuts, bolts, and washers	50
25.	Wheels and wheel clamps	16
26.	RF 433Mhz module	4
27.	Sensor compass	2
28.	Generic 2Pcs/Lot RGB proximity sensor	1
29.	Nano 3.0 controller compatible with Arduino Nano CH340 USB driver EDC-341848	1
30.	WIRELESS COMMUNICATION BOARD with ENCODER DECODER – HT12E and HT12D for RF module	2
31.	Generic BANGXECT3827 Ardokit smart robot car chassis kit speed encoder battery box for Arduino	2
32.	amiciKart Kit of 60W soldering iron + 5X bits of different shapes, temperature adjustable soldering iron handle heat pencil tool	1
33.	Stanley Gluepro trigger feed 69GR20B hot melt glue gun	1
34.	Generic 180–240V adjustable infrared IR body sensor switch module body moving detector	2
35.	Adapter – 2 amps for power supply to the power circuit, i.e. traffic light control system Adapter – 1 amp for power supply to the ambulance unit	2

- The Adafruit Unified Sensor Library (**Adafruit_Sensor**) provides a common interface and data type for any supported sensor. It defines some basic information about the sensor (sensor limits, etc.), and returns standard SI units of a specific kind and scale for each supported sensor type.

- It provides a simple abstraction layer between the application, and the actual sensor hardware allows any comparable sensor to be dropped in with only one or two lines of code to change in the project (essentially the constructor, since the functions to read sensor data and get information about the sensor are defined in the base Adafruit_Sensor class).

- The data can be used right away because it is already converted to SI units that we understand and can compare, rather than meaningless values like 0...1023.
- Because SI units are standardized in the sensor library, we can also do quick sanity checks working with new sensors, or drop in any comparable sensor if better sensitivity is needed or if a lower-cost unit becomes available, etc.

Adafruit HMC5883L Driver (3-Axis Magnetometer): This driver is for the Adafruit HMC5883L Breakout (http://www.adafruit.com/products/1746), and is based on Adafruit's Unified Sensor Library (Adafruit_Sensor). The HMC5883L is a digital (I2C) compass (magnetometer).

Import library for compass: To import library for magnetometer, follow the below steps.

- Step 1:
  - Click on "sketch".
  - Go to include library.
  - Click on manage library.
  - You will get a window, in which click on the filter tab.
  - Click the sensor number (HMC 5883L).
  - You will see the "Install" button on the right-hand side.
  - Click on Install.
- Step 2:
  - "Adafruit_sensor.h" header file to be pasted to the following folder:
  - Documents\Arduino\Libraries\Adafruit_HMC5883_Unified\Adafruit_Sensor.h
- **Compass Calibration Part**
  - Compass calibration is done at the ambulance module. This makes use of compass sensor data to find the direction of the ambulance. Accordingly, it writes "S" or "N" or "E" or "W" in serial port (UART). For example, serial.println("S"); puts the data "S" into UART. Then it is transmitted to the controller module via the Xbee pro module.

Number of serial ports (UART)	
TLS controller module/unit	**Ambulance robot module/unit**
4	1
(Arduino Mega ATMega 2560)	(Arduino Uno ATMega 328)

- Xbee pro module in TLS reads serial port to check whether it is "S" or "N" or "E" or "W". Accordingly, it switches on an appropriate signal to provide a way for the ambulance to move on and reverts to a regular signal after a certain delay.

- The below segment of code tests the reception of compass direction, i.e. ambulance direction, whether it is South or East or North or West.
  - *SOUTH*

    if((headingDegrees>= 150) && (headingDegrees<= 210))

    {mySerial.println('S');}
  - *EAST*

    If ((headingDegrees>= 60) && (headingDegrees<= 120))

    {mySerial.println('E');}
  - *NORTH*

    If ((((headingDegrees>= 0) && (headingDegrees<= 30)) || ((headingDegrees>= 330) && (headingDegrees<= 360)))

    {mySerial.println('N');}
  - *WEST*

    If ((headingDegrees>= 240) && (headingDegrees<= 300))

    {mySerial.println('W');}

7.4.4 Software Design and Coding

7.4.4.1 Traffic Light Control System Module

When an ambulance comes towards the north direction, the following code gets executed. To load the code into the hardware, follow the below steps.

- Click Tools menu.
- Choose port "COM68".
- Choose Board.
- Select "Arduino Mega/Genuino Mega (AT mega 2560).
- Check the port and then click upload.
- Click on serial monitor to see status in console in display.
- After uploading code to controller unit, remove USB data cable from the controller.

```
delay(1500);
digitalWrite(N_RED,LOW);
delay(1000);
digitalWrite(N_YELLOW,HIGH);
delay(2000);
digitalWrite(N_YELLOW,LOW);
digitalWrite(N_GREEN,HIGH);
delay(3000);
Serial1.flush();
  //Check for Xbee data
if(Serial1.available()>0)
{
if(Serial1.read() == 'N')
{
digitalWrite(N_GREEN,HIGH);
```

```
Serial.println("Changed to N-NORTH1");
                while (!((digitalRead(RF_inD3)==HIGH) &&
(digitalRead(RF_inD2)==LOW) && (digitalRead(RF_inD1)==LOW) &&
(digitalRead(RF_inD0)==LOW)));
Serial.println("RF In North");
delay(5000);
Serial.println("Ambulance Crossed NORTH");
Serial1.flush();
    }
if(Serial1.read() == 'S')
    {
digitalWrite(N_GREEN,LOW);
digitalWrite(N_RED,HIGH);
digitalWrite(S_RED,LOW);
digitalWrite(S_GREEN,HIGH);
Serial.println("Changed to N-SOUTH1");
while (!((digitalRead(RF_inD3)==HIGH) && (digitalRead(RF_inD2)==LOW)
&& (digitalRead(RF_inD1)==LOW) && (digitalRead(RF_inD0)==LOW)));
Serial.println("RF In South");
delay(5000);
Serial.println("Ambulance Crossed SOUTH");
Serial1.flush();
digitalWrite(S_RED,HIGH);
digitalWrite(S_GREEN,LOW);
digitalWrite(N_GREEN,HIGH);
digitalWrite(N_RED,LOW);
    }
if(Serial1.read() == 'E')
    {
digitalWrite(N_RED,HIGH);
digitalWrite(N_GREEN,LOW);
digitalWrite(E_RED,LOW);
digitalWrite(E_GREEN,HIGH);
Serial.println("Changed to N-EAST1");
while (!((digitalRead(RF_inD3)==HIGH) && (digitalRead(RF_inD2)==LOW)
&& (digitalRead(RF_inD1)==LOW) && (digitalRead(RF_inD0)==LOW)));
Serial.println("RF In EAST");
delay(5000);
Serial.println("Ambulance Crossed EAST");
Serial1.flush();
digitalWrite(E_GREEN,LOW);
digitalWrite(E_RED,HIGH);
digitalWrite(N_RED,LOW);
digitalWrite(N_GREEN,HIGH);
    }
if(Serial1.read() == 'W')
    {
digitalWrite(N_RED,HIGH);
digitalWrite(N_GREEN,LOW);
digitalWrite(W_RED,LOW);
digitalWrite(W_GREEN,HIGH);
Serial.println("Changed to N-WEST1");
while (!((digitalRead(RF_inD3)==HIGH) && (digitalRead(RF_inD2)==LOW)
&&(digitalRead(RF_inD1)==LOW) && (digitalRead(RF_inD0)==LOW)));
```

```
Serial.println("RF In WEST");
delay(5000);
Serial.println("Ambulance Crossed WEST");
Serial1.flush();
digitalWrite(W_RED,HIGH);
digitalWrite(W_GREEN,LOW);
digitalWrite(N_RED,LOW);
digitalWrite(N_GREEN,HIGH);
     }
}
Serial1.flush();
delay(3000);
digitalWrite(N_GREEN,LOW);
digitalWrite(N_RED,HIGH);
```

7.4.4.2 Ambulance Control System Module

The following operational steps have been carried out for the ambulance control system module.

- Compass calibration for correct direction identification.
- Read compass data and send to universal asynchronous receiver transmitter (UART). UART is a computer hardware device for asynchronous serial communication in which the data format and transmission speeds are configurable.
- Place the ambulance module on the prototype, so that Z is pointing "up" and we can measure the heading with the x and y of the compass fixed in the ambulance robot.
- Calculate heading when the magnetometer is level, then correct for signs of axis.
- Once it gets heading details, it must then add "Declination Angle", which is the "Error" of the magnetic field in the current location.
- Convert radians to degrees for readability.

To load the code into Arduino Uno hardware on the ambulance side, follow the below steps.

- Remove white and gray pair from Arduino Nano while uploading code to Arduino Nano. This cable goes from the Arduino Nano module to the Xbee module of the ambulance robot.
- Switch on "Power button" in Arduino board at Ambulance module.
- In the Tools menu, choose Board "Arduino Nano".
- Choose Port "COM70" or "COM60". The operating system will decide this.
- Processor "ATMega328".
- Check the port and then click upload.
- After uploading code, remove the USB data cable from the ambulance robot for safe disconnection.
- *Safe connection:*
- First, give power supply to both the ambulance and traffic light controller unit.

- Second, plug in USB data cable.
- *Safe disconnection:*
- First, remove the USB data cable.
- Then remove power cables.

```
void loop()
{
// Motor start
digitalWrite(Motor1p, LOW);
digitalWrite(Motor1n, HIGH);
digitalWrite(Motor2p, LOW);
digitalWrite(Motor2n, HIGH);
// Motor ends
// Blink start
digitalWrite(BlueLED1, HIGH);
digitalWrite(BlueLED2, LOW);
delay(100);
digitalWrite(BlueLED1, LOW);
digitalWrite(BlueLED2, HIGH);
delay(100);
// Blink ends
// Siren start
for (int z=0;z<5;z++)
{
delay(freq);
delay(freq);
delay(freq);
delay(freq);
delay(freq);
delay(freq);
if (loop_number>= 3)
{
loop_number = 0;
changeTone();
}
loop_number++;
//Siren ends
}
//Compass read & sends to UART (Universal Asynchronous Receiver
Transmitter)
sensors_event_t event;
mag.getEvent(&event);
// Hold the module so that Z is pointing "up" and you can measure the
heading with x and y
// Calculate heading when the magnetometer is level, then correct for
signs of axis.
float heading = atan2(event.magnetic.y, event.magnetic.x);
// Once you have your heading, you must then add your "Declination
Angle", which is the "Error" of the magnetic field in your location.
// Find yours here: http://www.magnetic-declination.com/
// Mine is: -13* 2' W, which is ~13 Degrees, or (which we need) 0.22
radians.
```

```
// If you cannot find your declination, comment out these two lines,
your compass will be slightly off.
floatdeclinationAngle = 0.22;
heading += declinationAngle;
// Correct for when signs are reversed.
if(heading < 0)
heading += 2*PI;
// Check for wrap due to addition of declination.
if(heading > 2*PI)
heading -= 2*PI;
// Convert radians to degrees for readability.
floatheadingDegrees = heading * 180/M_PI;
//Serial.print("Heading (degrees): ");
Serial.println(headingDegrees); //FOR CALLIBRATION
//delay(1000);//FOR CALLIBRATION
if((headingDegrees>= 150) && (headingDegrees<= 210))
{
mySerial.println('S');}//SOUTH
if((headingDegrees>= 60) && (headingDegrees<= 120))
{
mySerial.println('E');
}//EAST
if(((headingDegrees>= 0) && (headingDegrees<= 30)) ||
((headingDegrees>= 330) && (headingDegrees<= 360)))
{
mySerial.println('N');}//NORTH
if((headingDegrees>= 240) && (headingDegrees<= 300))
{
mySerial.println('W');
}//WEST
// Compass ends
//delay(2000);
//FOR CALLIBRATION
//RFmodule start
digitalWrite(RF_outD0,LOW);
digitalWrite(RF_outD1,LOW);
digitalWrite(RF_outD2,LOW);
digitalWrite(RF_outD3,HIGH);
delay(2000); //1500 reduced to 1 post after Ambulance is off, 2000 best
// RF module ends
}
}
voidchangeTone()
{
tone_number= !tone_number;
if (tone_number)
{
tone(Piezo_disc, lowNote, 1000);
    }
else
    {
tone(Piezo_disc, hiNote, 1000);
    }
}
```

7.4.4.3 Codes Download Constraints in Arduino, i.e. Uploading Coding into Arduino Board

- When downloading the code, ensure that you do not connect any device to Tx_0, and Rx_0 pins of Arduino Uno, Nano, Mega.
- For the real-time implementation of the project, we can use ATMEL studio or Embedded C.
- Programming can be done in two modes.
  - AT mode → simple
  - API mode → frame-based
- Traffic light control Xbee pro modem configuration
  - Networking → PAN ID must be the same in both traffic light control and ambulance control module.
  - Addressing → Destination address high is set to 0, and destination address low is set to 0.
  - After making changes, click on the "Write" button.
- Ambulance Xbee pro modem configuration
  - Networking → Channel verification – 1 ENABLED
  - Addressing → Destination address high is set to 0, and destination address low is set to 0
  - Then click on "write".

7.4.4.4 Device Driver Installation

- After connecting USB Cable, go to Control Panel → Device Manager
- USB 2.0 serial with the symbol → right-click on this
- Click on the update driver software
- Browse my computer folder ITS\Ch341scr → Click on this, Save → OK

7.4.4.5 Benefits of Intelligent Traffic Light Control System with Ambulance Control System

- Increases commuters safety
- Improves the operational performance of the Healthcare management system, particularly by enabling drivers to select the latent path with reduced congestion
- Enhances personal mobility and convenience
- Delivers environmental benefits
- Expand health benefits by granting early treatment for patients

7.4.4.6 Limitations of the Intelligent Traffic Light Control System with Ambulance Control System

- Traffic light system (TLS) scales up: The best way is to have a GPS module in the ambulance unit. GPS reading must be monitored from TLS to revert to normal signaling after the ambulance crosses the signal junction.

- In ambulance robot part:
  - The ambulance siren must be independent. Here is where more time is spent. We can use Melody IC, which comes with three sirens (police vehicle, ambulance vehicle, fire service vehicle).
  - Ambulance light (blue LED) may be controlled using 555 Timer IC in a stable multivibrator mode.
- Use of interrupt is suggested to check the correct reception of ambulance arrival signals through the XBee module.
- Arduino supports only serial port interrupts. However, it does not work correctly. It is a better choice to go with microcontrollers. When it comes to real-time implementation, Arduino boards must be replaced by PIC 18F series Microcontroller or DS PIC 32MX or ARM cortex series.
- Even when the ambulance module is switched off, the RF module still keeps sending signal data (direction data) to TLS controller. Potential solutions could be the following:
  - *Solution 1*: Impose delay of 1500–3000 m sec at ambulance module to transmit RF signal about ambulance arrival
  - *Solution 2*: Do flushing of data at RF receiver side which is available in TLS controller. A flush () function can be used after checking signal against GREEN LED.

7.5 Results and Discussion

Trichy is a metropolitan city which has seen a vast increase in the number of vehicles and traffic jams and suffers from a lack of footpaths. In Trichy, roads are unsafe for people who would like to walk or to cross roads. The transport authorities have given more importance to flyovers than to efficient public transport. Due to the unplanned growth of the city and the migration of people from rural areas and districts, an inefficient public transport system has resulted in an unpleasant situation for traffic in the city. In the last two decades, the number of vehicles has grown enormously. In Trichy, most people depend on personal vehicles for transport due to these traffic jams, and congestion on the streets has become quite common.

Figure 7.6 shows traffic jams are a familiar sight in the city. At present, there are about 11 lakhs (1.1 million) vehicles in the city. There has been a high growth rate in two-wheelers and cars during the last 5 years of the last decade, with an increased rate of about 10 percent per year. In Trichy, more than 80 percent of vehicles are two-wheelers (mostly two-stroke engines) producing a bulk amount of unborn hydrocarbons and carbon monoxide. About 10 percent of vehicles comprise trucks, buses, taxis, and three-wheelers, which are mostly used for daily transportation.

Transport vehicles used for commercial purposes (about 90,000) normally travel more than 100 km per day, and most of them are using diesel as fuel. More than 50 percent of these vehicles are reported to be not eligible or unfit for a PUC (pollution under control) certificate, as they are older than 15 years. The average life span of a vehicle is 6 years, which travels about 300 km per day and there is no way to use these kinds of vehicles after they have traveled for 500,000 km. Figure 7.7 shows the ambulance locations.

FIGURE 7.6
Traffic jams are a familiar sight in the city.

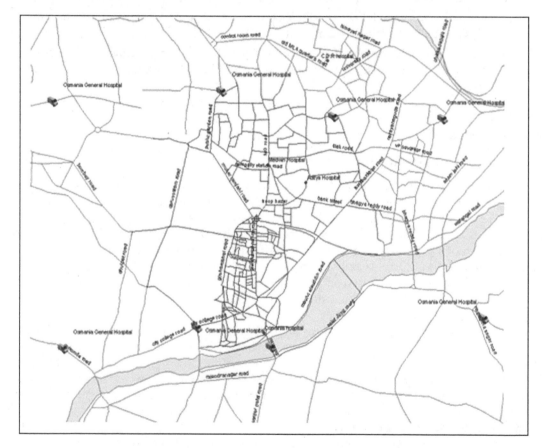

FIGURE 7.7
To identify ambulance locations.

Furthermore, Figure 7.8 shows the fastest route for all ambulances to the accident site. Figure 7.9 identifies the fastest routing ambulance to the accident. Figure 7.10 shows an alternate route during peak hours.

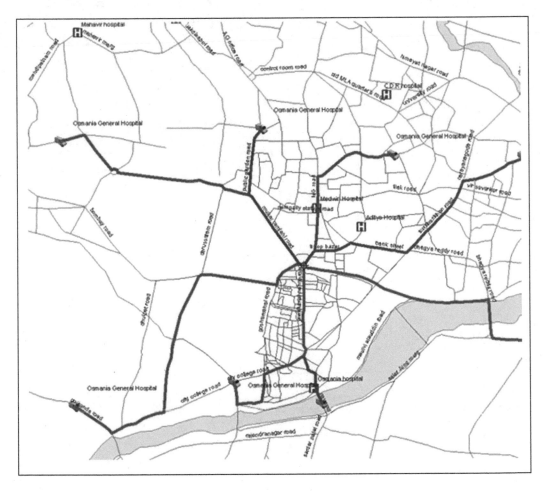

FIGURE 7.8
To identify the fastest route from all ambulances to the accident site.

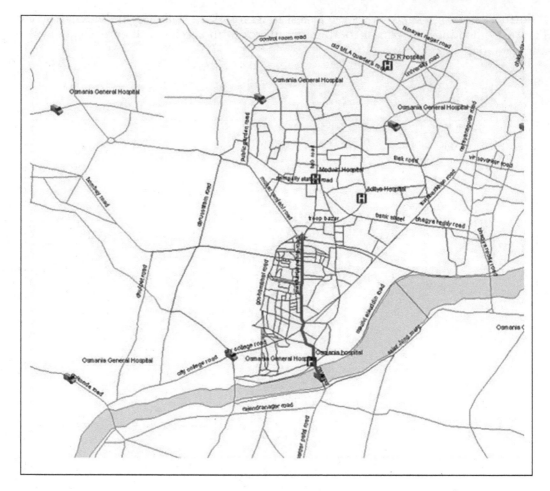

FIGURE 7.9
To identify the fastest routing ambulance to the accident.

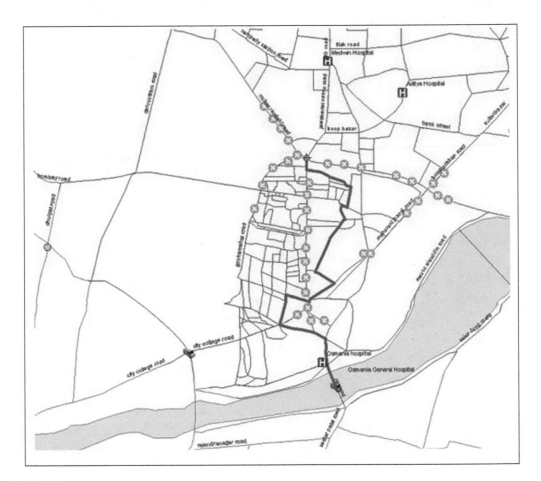

FIGURE 7.10
Alternate route during peak hours.

7.6 Summary

The Indian population and thereby the number of vehicles are increasing at the same time, causing congestion on road networks. The intelligent traffic light controller with ambulance control system (ITLC-ACS) is designed by analyzing the situation on the ground in any city, for example, the problems faced by the inhabitants while traveling on the road network, and in particular the difficulties faced by emergency service providers like hospitals during the transport of patients. ITLC-ACS plays a significant role in solving the routing problem of an ambulance on the road network when the need arises to transport a patient to the nearest hospital. Our ITLC-ACS significantly solves ambulance problems like determining the fastest routing for an ambulance. ITLC-ACS also analyzes those roads obstructed by congestion and other activities during peak hours and calculates the quickest route. ITLC-ACS is capable of handling a multi-accident situation.

8

Conclusions and Future Research

8.1 Conclusions

Traffic congestion is a significant problem, especially in growing nations, and to counter this, many models for traffic systems have been proposed. For a smart transportation system, a new framework, traffic prediction, is recommended to avoid congestion. The sample data is taken on an hourly volume in the low and moderate ranges, and a probability model and genetic prediction model for predicting traffic congestion and avoidance are established.

This prediction technique, along with a fuel consumption model, helps to avoid congestion and also reduces pollution, protects the green environment, and ensures safe travel. Based on the traffic flow structure pattern and regression method, short-term traffic flow can be predicted. The traffic flow at the subsequent time point can be predicted by using entrance flow information. The traffic flow over the course of a week is predicted using pattern information and locally weighted learning (LWL).

An efficient intelligent traffic light control and deviation (EITLCD) system is proposed to reduce the traffic congestion problem before it happens. This system will decrease traffic queue size and provide an alternative route for vehicles to avoid traffic and to achieve a free flow of vehicles. An intelligent traffic light control system is deployed to prevent traffic congestion before it occurs and, based on an alert signal, traffic will be diverted. This can ensure a free flow of traffic for travelers.

The significant contributions of this book are summarized below:

i. A smart traffic prediction and congestion avoidance system is proposed to enhance transportation services such as safe and secure travel, road safety, informed travel choices, efficient transportation, environmental protection, and traffic resilience. This system proposes predicting traffic congestion based on the arrival time of vehicles, thereby helping to reduce traffic congestion before it occurs. By diverting the vehicles via another route, traffic can be reduced. This will be effective at improving traffic conditions in the city, where the prediction can be made on the basis of vehicle arrival.

ii. Short-term traffic prediction is one of the required fields of study in the transportation domain. It would be beneficial to develop a more advanced transportation system to control traffic signals and avoid congestion. The proposed system for short-term traffic flow prediction is based on structure pattern and regression methods. Using a traffic flow structure pattern constructed from freeway toll data, it will improve the traffic system and thereby also protect the environment,

DOI: 10.1201/9781003217367-8

allowing rerouting, improving fuel consumption, and saving time. Based on the design, a prediction method was proposed which is based on LWL and regression.

iii. Traffic light control systems are widely used to monitor and control the flow of automobiles through junctions on many roads. Intelligent traffic light control is critical for an efficient transportation system. The proposed efficient intelligent traffic light control and deviation (EITLCD) system is based on a multi-agent system. It is composed of traffic light controller (TLC) and traffic light deviation (TLD) systems. The TLC system uses three agents to supervise and control the traffic parameters. The TLD system diverts the vehicles before they get onto the congested road. The EITLCD contains five elements: (i) Sensors: A magnetic sensor is chosen as a traffic sensor. (ii) Data collector agent: This examines the data collected via the sensors, detecting, counting, and categorizing the vehicles. (iii) Data processor agent: This determines vehicle length, velocity, and relative quantity of traffic. The data processor will manipulate the traffic data, and the input will be given to intelligent traffic light controller (TLC) system. (iv) Intelligent TLC: This supervisor agent controls the traffic signal. This system has a threshold value depending on the traffic area, and if the value exists, then an alert signal will be sent to the deviation system. (v) Intelligent TDS: If a congestion state is predicted, the deviation system gives a signal to divert the vehicles arriving on the congested route.

iv. An efficient smart intelligent transportation system (s-ITS) is made up of various components such as a central server, a radio frequency identification (RFID) device, sensors, a lighting control unit, and an EBOX II. The central server plays a significant role in providing resilience during any malfunctioning of the system. The RFID helps in communicating in data flow information between the cars and the EBOX II. This RFID device has tags and antennas to transmit information and readers to decode the data. It involves the smart building of the intelligent transport system with the ability to tackle real-time issues. The intelligent system is built to address the following modules: (i) Vehicular location tracking: This reduces the time required to select paths for the vehicles as well as providing easy location estimation. (ii) Intelligent vehicle parking system: Vehicle parking decisions are made based on outcome factors like whether a space is occupied or free. (iii) Communication within a VANET: The sensors track the location of the vehicle and its status in the current traffic scenario. (iv) Vehicular Big Data mining: Signals are communicated to the vehicles based on the mining of a huge volume of previous similar data and also on current traffic status.

v. To minimize the traffic problems typically faced by ambulances, an intelligent transport system is proposed. It integrates sensor information and communication technologies to achieve traffic efficiency, thereby improving environmental quality, conserving energy, saving time, and enhancing safety and comfort, especially for ambulance drivers. The proposed system has two modules which communicate with and are controlled by sophisticated hardware components: an intelligent traffic light control system and an ambulance control system.

The following operational steps are carried out in the ambulance control system:

- Compass calibration for correct direction identification.
- Read compass data and send to a universal asynchronous receiver transmitter (UART). UART is a computer hardware device for asynchronous serial communication in which the data format and transmission speeds are configurable.

- Place the ambulance module on the prototype, so that Z is pointing "up" and can measure the heading with x and y of a compass installed in the ambulance robot.
- Calculate heading when the magnetometer is level, then correct for signs of the axis.

8.2 Scope for Future Research

These proposed works are instrumental in solving ambulance routing problems, and in future they can also be used by other emergency service providers. This same prototype can be used by the police and fire authorities to perform the following functionalities.

- To find the nearest and fastest route from the police vehicle to the crime scene; it would also be helpful in finding the crime scene area on the digital city map, and even the route back to the nearest police station.
- To find the location of a fire on a digital map and alert the fire vehicles on the fastest route to reach the fire location.

Bibliography

Abadi, A, Rajabioun, T & Ioannou, PA 2014, 'Traffic flow prediction for road transportation networks with limited traffic data', *IEEE Transactions on Intelligent Transportation Systems*, vol. 16, no. 2, pp. 653–662.

Abdalla, A & Abaker, M 2016, 'A survey on automobile collision avoidance system', *International Journal of Recent Trends in Engineering & Research*, vol. 2, no. 6, pp. 1–6.

Abdulhai, B, Porwal, H & Recker, W 2002, 'Short-term traffic flow prediction using neuro-genetic algorithms', *ITS Journal-Intelligent Transportation Systems Journal*, vol. 7, no. 1, pp. 3–41.

Aceves, SM & Paddack, E 2002, *Developing Intelligent Transportation Systems in an Integrated Systems Analysis Environment*, Lawrence Livermore National Lab.

Agarwal, Y, Jain, K & Karabasoglu, O 2018, 'Smart vehicle monitoring and assistance using cloud computing in vehicular Ad Hoc networks', *International Journal of Transportation Science and Technology*, vol. 7, no. 1, pp. 60–73.

Ahmed, MS & Cook, AR 1979, 'Analysis of freeway traffic time-series data by using Box-Jenkins techniques', *Transportation Research Record*, no. 722, pp. 1–9.

Ali, SSM, George, B, Vanajakshi, L & Venkatraman, J 2011, 'A multiple inductive loop vehicle detection system for heterogeneous and lane-less traffic', *IEEE Transactions on Instrumentation and Measurement*, vol. 61, no. 5, pp. 1353–1360.

Alsrehin, NO, Klaib, AF & Magableh, A 2019, 'Intelligent transportation and control systems using data mining and machine learning techniques: A comprehensive study', *IEEE Access*, vol. 7, pp. 49830–49857.

Angelidou, M 2015, 'Smart cities: A conjuncture of four forces', *Cities*, vol. 47, pp. 95–106.

Atkeson, CG, Moore, AW & Schaal, S 1997, 'Locally weighted learning for control', in *Lazy Learning*, Springer, pp. 75–113.

Atta, A, Abbas, S, Khan, MA, Ahmed, G & Farooq, U 2018, 'An adaptive approach: Smart traffic congestion control system', *Journal of King Saud University-Computer and Information Sciences*, vol. 32, no. 9, pp. 1012–1019.

Aziz, S, Hayat, S, Hammadi, S & Borne, P 1999, 'New strategy for the aid decision-making based on the fuzzy inferences in the traffic regulation of an urban bus network', in Proceedings of the IEEE International Conference on Systems, Man, and Cybernetics (IEEE SMC'99) (Cat. No. 99CH37028), vol. 6, pp. 1069–1073. Tokyo, Japan.

Barimani, N, Kian, AR & Moshiri, B 2014, 'Real time adaptive non-linear estimator/predictor design for traffic systems with inadequate detectors', *IET Intelligent Transport Systems*, vol. 8, no. 3, pp. 308–321.

Bojan, TM, Kumar, UR & Bojan, VM 2014, 'An internet of things based intelligent transportation system', in IEEE International Conference on Vehicular Electronics and Safety, pp. 174–179. Hyderabad, India.

Bowman, CN & Miller, JA 2016, 'Modeling traffic flow using simulation and big data analytics', in Winter Simulation Conference (WSC), pp. 1206–1217. Arlington, Virginia.

Buscema, M 1998, 'Back propagation neural networks', *Substance Use & Misuse*, vol. 33, no. 2, pp. 233–270.

Cai, Y, Zhang, W & Wang, H 2010, 'Measurement of vehicle queue length based on video processing in intelligent traffic signal control system', in International Conference on Measuring Technology and Mechatronics Automation, vol. 2, pp. 615–618. Changsha, China.

Chen, C, Petty, K, Skabardonis, A, Varaiya, P & Jia, Z 2001, 'Freeway performance measurement system: Mining loop detector data', *Transportation Research Record*, vol. 1748, no. 1, pp. 96–102.

Cheung, SY, Coleri, S, Dundar, B, Ganesh, S, Tan, C-W & Varaiya, P 2005, 'Traffic measurement and vehicle classification with single magnetic sensor', *Transportation Research Record*, vol. 1917, no. 1, pp. 173–181.

Chiu, S & Chand, S 1993, 'Self-organizing traffic control via fuzzy logic', in Proceedings of the 32nd IEEE Conference on Decision and Control, pp. 1897–1902. San Antonio, Texas.

Chrobok, R, Wahle, J & Schreckenberg, M 2001, 'Traffic forecast using simulations of large scale networks', in Proceedings of the IEEE Intelligent Transportation Systems (ITSC) (Cat. No. 01TH8585), pp. 434–439.

Coifman, B 2001, 'Improved velocity estimation using single loop detectors', *Transportation Research Part A: Policy and Practice*, vol. 35, no. 10, pp. 863–880.

Costa, E & Seixas, J 2014, 'Contribution of electric cars to the mitigation of CO_2 emissions in the city of São Paulo', in IEEE Vehicle Power and Propulsion Conference (VPPC), pp. 1–5.

Cui, F 2010, 'Study of traffic flow prediction based on BP neural network', in 2nd International Workshop on Intelligent Systems and Applications, pp. 1–4. Wuhan, China.

de la Garza, J, Taylor, C & Sinha, S 2013, 'An integrated framework and smart algorithm for vehicle localization in intelligent transportation systems', pp. 2–115.

De Lima, GRT, Silva, JDS & Saotome, O 2010, 'Vehicle inductive signatures recognition using a Madaline neural network', *Neural Computing and Applications*, vol. 19, no. 3, pp. 421–436.

de Paula, LC, Soares, AS, de Lima, TW & Coelho, CJ 2016, 'Feature selection using genetic algorithm: An analysis of the bias-property for one-point crossover', in Proceedings of the Genetic and Evolutionary Computation Conference Companion, pp. 1461–1462. Denver, Colorado.

Do, LN, Vu, HL, Vo, BQ, Liu, Z & Phung, D 2019, 'An effective spatial-temporal attention based neural network for traffic flow prediction', *Transportation Research Part C: Emerging Technologies*, vol. 108, pp. 12–28.

Fallah, YP & Khandani, MK 2016, 'Context and network aware communication strategies for connected vehicle safety applications', *IEEE Intelligent Transportation Systems Magazine*, vol. 8, no. 4, pp. 92–101.

Fay, A & Schnieder, E 1999, 'Knowledge-based decision support system for real-time train traffic control', in *Computer-Aided Transit Scheduling*, Springer, pp. 347–370.

Garib, A, Radwan, A & Al-Deek, H 1997, 'Estimating magnitude and duration of incident delays', *Journal of Transportation Engineering*, vol. 123, no. 6, pp. 459–466.

Gaur, A, Scotney, BW, Parr, GP & McClean, SI 2015, 'Smart city architecture and its applications based on IoT', in ANT/SEIT, pp. 1089–1094.

Grob, GR 2009, 'Future transportation with smart grids & sustainable energy', in 6th International Multi-Conference on Systems, Signals and Devices, pp. 1–5.

Grubb, H & Mason, A 2001, 'Long lead-time forecasting of UK air passengers by Holt–Winters methods with damped trend', *International Journal of Forecasting*, vol. 17, no. 1, pp. 71–82.

Guerrero-Ibáñez, J, Zeadally, S & Contreras-Castillo, J 2018, 'Sensor technologies for intelligent transportation systems', *Sensors*, vol. 18, no. 4, pp. 1212.

Guo, J, Huang, W & Williams, BM 2014, 'Adaptive Kalman filter approach for stochastic short-term traffic flow rate prediction and uncertainty quantification', *Transportation Research Part C: Emerging Technologies*, vol. 43, pp. 50–64.

Habtemichael, FG & Cetin, M 2016, 'Short-term traffic flow rate forecasting based on identifying similar traffic patterns', *Transportation Research Part C: Emerging Technologies*, vol. 66, pp. 61–78.

Hair, JF, Black, WC, Babin, BJ, Anderson, RE & Tatham, RL 1998, *Multivariate Data Analysis*, vol. 5, Prentice Hall.

Hair, William, Barry & Rolphe 2010, *Multivariate Data Analysis*, Pearson Publication, pp. 4–761.

Hamidi, H & Kamankesh, A 2018, 'An approach to intelligent traffic management system using a multi-agent system', *International Journal of Intelligent Transportation Systems Research*, vol. 16, no. 2, pp. 112–124.

Han, L, Wu, J, Gu, P, Xie, K, Song, G, Tang, S, Yang, D, Jiao, B & Gao, F 2010, 'Adaptive knowledge transfer based on locally weighted learning', in International Conference on Technologies and Applications of Artificial Intelligence, pp. 392–397. Hsinchu City, Taiwan.

Harilakshmi, V & Rani, PAJ 2016, 'Intelligent vehicle counter-a road to sustainable development and pollution prevention (P2)', in 2016 International Conference on Energy Efficient Technologies for Sustainability (ICEETS), pp. 877–880. Nagercoil, India.

Hartenstein, H & Laberteaux, K 2009, *VANET: Vehicular Applications and Inter-networking Technologies*, vol. 1, Wiley.

Hegyi, A, De Schutter, B, Hoogendoorn, S, Babuska, R, van Zuylen, H & Schuurman, H 2001, 'A fuzzy decision support system for traffic control centers', in Proceedings of the IEEE Intelligent Transportation Systems (ITSC) (Cat. No. 01TH8585), pp. 358–363.

Hochreiter, S & Schmidhuber, J 1997, 'Long short-term memory', *Neural Computation*, vol. 9, no. 8, pp. 1735–1780.

Holland, J 1975, 'Adaptation in natural and artificial systems: An introductory analysis with application to biology', control and artificial intelligence', in *Adaptation in Natural and Artificial Systems*, first edition. Ann Arbor: University of Michigan Press.

Hou, Q, Leng, J, Ma, G, Liu, W & Cheng, Y 2019, 'An adaptive hybrid model for short-term urban traffic flow prediction', *Physica A: Statistical Mechanics and its Applications*, vol. 527, pp. 121065.

Houbraken, M, Logghe, S, Schreuder, M, Audenaert, P, Colle, D & Pickavet, M 2017, 'Automated incident detection using real-time floating car data', *Journal of Advanced Transportation*, vol. 2017, pp. 1–13.

Huang, D-Y, Chen, C-H, Hu, W-C, Yi, S-C & Lin, Y-F 2012, 'Feature-based vehicle flow analysis and measurement for a real-time traffic surveillance system', *Journal of Information Hiding and Multimedia Signal Processing*, vol. 3, no. 3, pp. 279–294.

Huang, W, Song, G, Hong, H & Xie, K 2014, 'Deep architecture for traffic flow prediction: Deep belief networks with multitask learning', *IEEE Transactions on Intelligent Transportation Systems*, vol. 15, no. 5, pp. 2191–2201.

Hunter, T, Herring, R, Abbeel, P & Bayen, A 2009, 'Path and travel time inference from GPS probe vehicle data', *NIPS Analyzing Networks and Learning with Graphs*, vol. 12, no. 1, pp. 2.

Iscaro, G & Nakamiti, G 2013, 'A supervisor agent for urban traffic monitoring', in IEEE International Multi-Disciplinary Conference on Cognitive Methods in Situation Awareness and Decision Support (CogSIMA), pp. 167–170. San Diego, California.

Iturrate, M, Gurrutxaga, I, López-de-Ipiña, K, Oses, U & Calvo, P 2015, 'Sustainable transport at the university of the basque country in San Sebastian', in 4th International Work Conference on Bioinspired Intelligence (IWOBI), pp. 15–20. San Sebastian, Spain.

Jeong, Y-S, Byon, Y-J, Castro-Neto, MM & Easa, SM 2013, 'Supervised weighting-online learning algorithm for short-term traffic flow prediction', *IEEE Transactions on Intelligent Transportation Systems*, vol. 14, no. 4, pp. 1700–1707.

Jiang, X, Zhang, L & Chen, XM 2014, 'Short-term forecasting of high-speed rail demand: A hybrid approach combining ensemble empirical mode decomposition and gray support vector machine with real-world applications in China', *Transportation Research Part C: Emerging Technologies*, vol. 44, pp. 110–127.

Jiber, M, Lamouik, I, Ali, Y & Sabri, MA 2018, 'Traffic flow prediction using neural network', in International Conference on Intelligent Systems and Computer Vision (ISCV), pp. 1–4. Fez, Morocco.

Jin, C, Wei, DX & Low, SH 2004, 'FAST TCP: Motivation, architecture, algorithms, performance', in IEEE INFOCOM, vol. 4, pp. 2490–2501.

Karlaftis, MG & Vlahogianni, EI 2011, 'Statistical methods versus neural networks in transportation research: Differences, similarities and some insights', *Transportation Research Part C: Emerging Technologies*, vol. 19, no. 3, pp. 387–399.

Khajenasiri, I, Estebsari, A, Verhelst, M & Gielen, G 2017, 'A review on Internet of Things solutions for intelligent energy control in buildings for smart city applications', *Energy Procedia*, vol. 111, pp. 770–779.

Khandelwal, I, Adhikari, R & Verma, G 2015, 'Time series forecasting using hybrid ARIMA and ANN models based on DWT decomposition', *Procedia Computer Science*, vol. 48, no. 1, pp. 173–179.

Ki, Y-K & Baik, D-K 2006, 'Vehicle-classification algorithm for single-loop detectors using neural networks', *IEEE Transactions on Vehicular Technology*, vol. 55, no. 6, pp. 1704–1711.

Kim, T-h, Ramos, C & Mohammed, S 2017, *Smart City and IoT*, Elsevier, pp. 0167–739X.

Kim, W & Chang, G-L 2012, 'Development of a hybrid prediction model for freeway incident duration: A case study in Maryland', *International Journal of Intelligent Transportation Systems Research*, vol. 10, no. 1, pp. 22–33.

Kim, W, Chang, G-L & Rochon, SM 2008, 'Analysis of freeway incident duration for atis applications', in Proceedings of the 15th World Congress on Intelligent Transport Systems and ITS America Annual Meeting, pp. 950–958. New York.

Ko, E, Ahn, J & Kim, EY 2016, '3D Markov process for traffic flow prediction in real-time', *Sensors*, vol. 16, no. 2, pp. 147.

Koesdwiady, A, Soua, R & Karray, F 2016, 'Improving traffic flow prediction with weather information in connected cars: A deep learning approach', *IEEE Transactions on Vehicular Technology*, vol. 65, no. 12, pp. 9508–9517.

Kumar, SV 2017, 'Traffic flow prediction using Kalman filtering technique', *Procedia Engineering*, vol. 187, pp. 582–587.

Kumar, SV &Vanajakshi, L 2015, 'Short-term traffic flow prediction using seasonal ARIMA model with limited input data', *European Transport Research Review*, vol. 7, no. 3, pp. 21.

Kummitha, RKR & Crutzen, N 2017, 'How do we understand smart cities? An evolutionary perspective', *Cities*, vol. 67, pp. 43–52.

Kyriazis, D & Varvarigou, T 2013, 'Smart, autonomous and reliable Internet of Things', *Procedia Computer Science*, vol. 21, pp. 442–448.

Lamas-Seco, JJ, Castro, PM, Dapena, A & Vazquez-Araujo, FJ 2015, 'Vehicle classification using the discrete fourier transform with traffic inductive sensors', *Sensors*, vol. 15, no. 10, pp. 27201–27214.

Lamini, C, Benhlima, S & Elbekri, A 2018, 'Genetic algorithm based approach for autonomous mobile robot path planning', *Procedia Computer Science*, vol. 127, no. C, pp. 180–189.

Lee, S, Krammes, RA & Yen, J 1998, 'Fuzzy-logic-based incident detection for signalized diamond interchanges', *Transportation Research Part C: Emerging Technologies*, vol. 6, no. 5–6, pp. 359–377.

Lee, Y & Wei, CH 2010, 'A computerized feature selection method using genetic algorithms to forecast freeway accident duration times', *Computer-Aided Civil and Infrastructure Engineering*, vol. 25, no. 2, pp. 132–148.

Li, X, Li, M, Gong, Y-J, Zhang, X-L & Yin, J 2016, 'T-DesP: Destination prediction based on big trajectory data', *IEEE Transactions on Intelligent Transportation Systems*, vol. 17, no. 8, pp. 2344–2354.

Lin, L, Li, J, Chen, F, Ye, J & Huai, J 2017, 'Road traffic speed prediction: A probabilistic model fusing multi-source data', *IEEE Transactions on Knowledge and Data Engineering*, vol. 30, no. 7, pp. 1310–1323.

Lippi, M, Bertini, M & Frasconi, P 2013, 'Short-term traffic flow forecasting: An experimental comparison of time-series analysis and supervised learning', *IEEE Transactions on Intelligent Transportation Systems*, vol. 14, no. 2, pp. 871–882.

Liu, H, Taniguchi, T, Tanaka, Y, Takenaka, K & Bando, T 2017, 'Visualization of driving behavior based on hidden feature extraction by using deep learning', *IEEE Transactions on Intelligent Transportation Systems*, vol. 18, no. 9, pp. 2477–2489.

Liu, HX, He, X & Recker, W 2007, 'Estimation of the time-dependency of values of travel time and its reliability from loop detector data', *Transportation Research Part B: Methodological*, vol. 41, no. 4, pp. 448–461.

Liu, X, Fang, X, Qin, Z, Ye, C & Xie, M 2011, 'A short-term forecasting algorithm for network traffic based on chaos theory and SVM', *Journal of Network and Systems Management*, vol. 19, no. 4, pp. 427–447.

Liu, Y & Wang, R 2016, 'Study on network traffic forecast model of SVR optimized by GAFSA', *Chaos, Solitons & Fractals*, vol. 89, pp. 153–159.

Liu, Z, Li, Z, Li, M, Xing, W & Lu, D 2016, 'Mining road network correlation for traffic estimation via compressive sensing', *IEEE Transactions on Intelligent Transportation Systems*, vol. 17, no. 7, pp. 1880–1893.

Lopez-Garcia, P, Onieva, E, Osaba, E, Masegosa, AD & Perallos, A 2015, 'A hybrid method for short-term traffic congestion forecasting using genetic algorithms and cross entropy', *IEEE Transactions on Intelligent Transportation Systems*, vol. 17, no. 2, pp. 557–569.

Lu, H-p, Sun, Z-y, Qu, W-c & Wang, L 2015, 'Real-time corrected traffic correlation model for traffic flow forecasting', *Mathematical Problems in Engineering*, vol. 2015, pp. 1–7.

Luo, X, Li, D & Zhang, S 2019, 'Traffic flow prediction during the holidays based on DFT and SVR', *Journal of Sensors*, vol. 2019, pp. 1–10.

Lv, Y, Duan, Y, Kang, W, Li, Z & Wang, F-Y 2014, 'Traffic flow prediction with big data: A deep learning approach', *IEEE Transactions on Intelligent Transportation Systems*, vol. 16, no. 2, pp. 865–873.

Ma, X, Dai, Z, He, Z, Ma, J, Wang, Y & Wang, Y 2017, 'Learning traffic as images: A deep convolutional neural network for large-scale transportation network speed prediction', *Sensors*, vol. 17, no. 4, pp. 818.

Ma, X, Tao, Z, Wang, Y, Yu, H & Wang, Y 2015, 'Long short-term memory neural network for traffic speed prediction using remote microwave sensor data', *Transportation Research Part C: Emerging Technologies*, vol. 54, pp. 187–197.

Mehar, S, Zeadally, S, Remy, G & Senouci, SM 2014, 'Sustainable transportation management system for a fleet of electric vehicles', *IEEE Transactions on Intelligent Transportation Systems*, vol. 16, no. 3, pp. 1401–1414.

Migliavacca, M & Cugola, G 2007, 'Adapting publish-subscribe routing to traffic demands', in Proceedings of the Inaugural International Conference on Distributed Event-based Systems, pp. 91–96.

Mohamed, A-r, Sainath, TN, Dahl, G, Ramabhadran, B, Hinton, GE & Picheny, MA 2011, 'Deep belief networks using discriminative features for phone recognition', in IEEE International Conference on Acoustics, Speech and Signal Processing (ICASSP), pp. 5060–5063.

Montero, L, Codina, E, Barceló, J & Barceló, P 1998, 'Combining macroscopic and microscopic approaches for transportation planning and design of road networks', in Proceedings of the 19th ARRB Meeting, Sydney.

Nair, AS, Liu, J-C, Rilett, L & Gupta, S 2001, 'Non-linear analysis of traffic flow', in Proceedings of the IEEE Intelligent Transportation Systems (ITSC) (Cat. No. 01TH8585), pp. 681–685.

Niu, X, Zhu, Y, Cao, Q, Zhang, X, Xie, W & Zheng, K 2015, 'An online-traffic-prediction based route finding mechanism for smart city', *International Journal of Distributed Sensor Networks*, vol. 11, no. 8, pp. 970256.

Okutani, I & Stephanedes, YJ 1984, 'Dynamic prediction of traffic volume through Kalman filtering theory', *Transportation Research Part B: Methodological*, vol. 18, no. 1, pp. 1–11.

Omkar, G & Kumar, SV 2017, 'Time series decomposition model for traffic flow forecasting in urban midblock sections', in International Conference On Smart Technologies For Smart Nation (SmartTechCon), pp. 720–723.

Osorio, C & Nanduri, K 2015, 'Energy-efficient urban traffic management: A microscopic simulation-based approach', *Transportation Science*, vol. 49, no. 3, pp. 637–651.

Pan, B, Demiryurek, U & Shahabi, C 2018, 'Traffic prediction using real-world transportation data', U.S. Patent 9,996,798, issued June 12, 2018.

Park, S-h, Kim, S-m & Ha, Y-g 2016, 'Highway traffic accident prediction using VDS big data analysis', *The Journal of Supercomputing*, vol. 72, no. 7, pp. 2815–2831.

Perera, C, Zaslavsky, A, Christen, P & Georgakopoulos, D 2013, 'Context aware computing for the internet of things: A survey', *IEEE Communications Surveys & Tutorials*, vol. 16, no. 1, pp. 414–454.

Petracca, M, Pagano, P, Pelliccia, R, Ghibaudi, M, Salvadori, C & Nastasi, C 2013, 'On-Board Unit hardware and software design for Vehicular Ad-hoc Networks', in *Roadside Networks for Vehicular Communications: Architectures, Applications, and Test Fields*, IGI Global, pp. 38–56.

Petrov, T, Dado, M & Ambrosch, KE 2017, 'Computer modelling of cooperative intelligent transportation systems', *Procedia Engineering*, vol. 192, pp. 683–688.

Pfeifer, PE & Deutsch, SJ 1980, 'Identification and interpretation of first order space-time ARMA models', *Technometrics*, vol. 22, no. 3, pp. 397–408.

Raj, J, Bahuleyan, H & Vanajakshi, LD 2016, 'Application of data mining techniques for traffic density estimation and prediction', *Transportation Research Procedia*, vol. 17, pp. 321–330.

Raza, A & Zhong, M 2017, 'Hybrid lane-based short-term urban traffic speed forecasting: A genetic approach', in 4th International Conference on Transportation Information and Safety (ICTIS), pp. 271–279. Banff, Alberta.

Rice, J & Van Zwet, E 2004, 'A simple and effective method for predicting travel times on freeways', *IEEE Transactions on Intelligent Transportation Systems*, vol. 5, no. 3, pp. 200–207.

Sadek, AW, Demetsky, MJ & Smith, BL 1999, 'Case-based reasoning for real-time traffic flow management', *Computer-Aided Civil and Infrastructure Engineering*, vol. 14, no. 5, pp. 347–356.

Saini, T, Sinha, A & Srikanth, S 2015, 'Urban travel demand estimation using genetic algorithm', in International Conference on Cognitive Computing and Information Processing (CCIP), pp. 1–6. Noida, India.

Salama, AS, Saleh, BK & Eassa, MM 2010, 'Intelligent cross road traffic management system (ICRTMS)', in 2nd International Conference on Computer Technology and Development, pp. 27–31. Cairo, Egypt.

Samadi, S, Rad, AP, Kazemi, FM & Jafarian, H 2012, 'Performance evaluation of intelligent adaptive traffic control systems: A case study', *Journal of Transportation Technologies*, vol. 2, no. 3, pp. 248.

Schrank, D, Eisele, B & Lomax, T 2015, *2014 Urban Mobility Report: Powered by Inrix Traffic Data*. No. SWUTC/15/161302-1. 2015.

Shandiz, HT, Khosravi, M & Doaee, M 2009, 'Intelligent transport system based on genetic algorithm', *World Applied Sciences Journal*, vol. 6, no. 7, pp. 908–913.

Sheng-nan, L, Pei-pei, D, Jian-li, F & Xiao-he, L 2015, 'The implementation of intelligent transportation system based on the internet of things', *Journal of Chemical and Pharmaceutical Research*, vol. 7, no. 3, pp. 1074–1077.

Sherly, J & Somasundareswari, D 2015, 'Internet of things based smart transportation systems', *International Research Journal of Engineering and Technology*, vol. 2, no. 7, pp. 1207–1210.

Smith, BL & Demetsky, MJ 1994, 'Short-term traffic flow prediction models-a comparison of neural network and nonparametric regression approaches', in *Proceedings of IEEE International Conference on Systems, Man and Cybernetics*, vol. 2, pp. 1706–1709. San Antonio, Texas.

Sta, HB 2017, 'Quality and the efficiency of data in "Smart-Cities"', *Future Generation Computer Systems*, vol. 74, pp. 409–416.

Stathopoulos, A & Karlaftis, MG 2003, 'A multivariate state space approach for urban traffic flow modeling and prediction', *Transportation Research Part C: Emerging Technologies*, vol. 11, no. 2, pp. 121–135.

Sun, H, Liu, HX, Xiao, H, He, RR & Ran, B 2003, 'Use of local linear regression model for short-term traffic forecasting', *Transportation Research Record*, vol. 1836, no. 1, pp. 143–150.

Sun, S, Yu, G & Zhang, C 2004, 'Short-term traffic flow forecasting using sampling Markov Chain method with incomplete data', in IEEE Intelligent Vehicles Symposium, pp. 437–441.

Sun, S, Zhang, C & Yu, G 2006, 'A Bayesian network approach to traffic flow forecasting', *IEEE Transactions on Intelligent Transportation Systems*, vol. 7, no. 1, pp. 124–132.

Taghvaeeyan, S & Rajamani, R 2013, 'Portable roadside sensors for vehicle counting, classification, and speed measurement', *IEEE Transactions on Intelligent Transportation Systems*, vol. 15, no. 1, pp. 73–83.

Tang, J, Liu, F, Zhang, W, Ke, R & Zou, Y 2018, 'Lane-changes prediction based on adaptive fuzzy neural network', *Expert Systems with Applications*, vol. 91, pp. 452–463.

Tang, J, Liu, F, Zou, Y, Zhang, W & Wang, Y 2017, 'An improved fuzzy neural network for traffic speed prediction considering periodic characteristic', *IEEE Transactions on Intelligent Transportation Systems*, vol. 18, no. 9, pp. 2340–2350.

Tom Tom. 2015. Available from: <https://corporate.tomtom.com/news-releases> [11 October 2018].

Tong, M & Tang, M 2010, 'LEACH-B: An improved LEACH protocol for wireless sensor network', in 6th International Conference on Wireless Communications Networking and Mobile Computing (WiCOM), pp. 1–4. Chengdu, China.

Valenti, G, Lelli, M & Cucina, D 2010, 'A comparative study of models for the incident duration prediction', *European Transport Research Review*, vol. 2, no. 2, pp. 103–111.

Van Der Voort, M, Dougherty, M & Watson, S 1996, 'Combining Kohonen maps with ARIMA time series models to forecast traffic flow', *Transportation Research Part C: Emerging Technologies*, vol. 4, no. 5, pp. 307–318.

Van Lint, J, Hoogendoorn, S & van Zuylen, HJ 2002, 'Freeway travel time prediction with state-space neural networks: Modeling state-space dynamics with recurrent neural networks', *Transportation Research Record*, vol. 1811, no. 1, pp. 30–39.

Vanajakshi, L, Ramadurai, G & Anand, A 2010, 'Intelligent transportation systems: Synthesis report on its including issues and challenges in india', Centre of Excellence in Urban Transport, Indian Institute of Technology Madras, December 2010.

Vandewater, L, Brusic, V, Wilson, W, Macaulay, L & Zhang, P 2015, 'An adaptive genetic algorithm for selection of blood-based biomarkers for prediction of Alzheimer's disease progression', *BMC Bioinformatics*, vol. 16, no. 18, Supplement 18, pp. S1.

Vlahogianni, EI & Karlaftis, MG 2013, 'Fuzzy-entropy neural network freeway incident duration modeling with single and competing uncertainties', *Computer-Aided Civil and Infrastructure Engineering*, vol. 28, no. 6, pp. 420–433.

Vlahogianni, EI, Karlaftis, MG & Golias, JC 2008, 'Temporal evolution of short-term urban traffic flow: A nonlinear dynamics approach', *Computer-Aided Civil and Infrastructure Engineering*, vol. 23, no. 7, pp. 536–548.

Vlahogianni, EI, Karlaftis, MG & Golias, JC 2014, 'Short-term traffic forecasting: Where we are and where we're going', *Transportation Research Part C: Emerging Technologies*, vol. 43, pp. 3–19.

Wang, M, Liang, H, Zhang, R, Deng, R & Shen, X 2014, 'Mobility-aware coordinated charging for electric vehicles in VANET-enhanced smart grid', *IEEE Journal on Selected Areas in Communications*, vol. 32, no. 7, pp. 1344–1360.

Wang, S, Li, R & Guo, M 2018, 'Application of nonparametric regression in predicting traffic incident duration', *Transport*, vol. 33, no. 1, pp. 22–31.

Wang, Y, Li, L & Xu, X 2017, 'A piecewise hybrid of ARIMA and SVMs for short-term traffic flow prediction', in International Conference on Neural Information Processing, pp. 493–502.

Wei, C-H & Lee, Y 2007, 'Sequential forecast of incident duration using artificial neural network models', *Accident Analysis & Prevention*, vol. 39, no. 5, pp. 944–954.

Weil, R, Wootton, J & Garcia-Ortiz, A 1998, 'Traffic incident detection: Sensors and algorithms', *Mathematical and Computer Modelling*, vol. 27, no. 9–11, pp. 257–291.

Wen, H, Yang, Z, Jiang, G & Shao, C 2001, 'A new algorithm of incident detection on freeways', in Proceedings of the IEEE International Vehicle Electronics Conference (IVEC) (Cat. No. 01EX522), pp. 197–202.

Williams, BM & Hoel, LA 2003, 'Modeling and forecasting vehicular traffic flow as a seasonal ARIMA process: Theoretical basis and empirical results', *Journal of Transportation Engineering*, vol. 129, no. 6, pp. 664–672.

Xu, H, Kwan, C, Haynes, L & Pryor, J 1998, 'Real-time adaptive on-line traffic incident detection', *Fuzzy Sets and Systems*, vol. 93, no. 2, pp. 173–183.

Yao, B, Chen, C, Cao, Q, Jin, L, Zhang, M, Zhu, H & Yu, B 2017, 'Short-term traffic speed prediction for an urban corridor', *Computer-Aided Civil and Infrastructure Engineering*, vol. 32, no. 2, pp. 154–169.

Yeh, C-H, Deng, H & Chang, Y-H 2000, 'Fuzzy multicriteria analysis for performance evaluation of bus companies', *European Journal of Operational Research*, vol. 126, no. 3, pp. 459–473.

Yi, H, Jung, H & Bae, S 2017, 'Deep neural networks for traffic flow prediction', in IEEE International Conference on Big Data and Smart Computing (BigComp), pp. 328–331.

Yin, L, He, Y, Dong, X & Lu, Z 2012, 'Multi-step prediction of Volterra neural network for traffic flow based on chaos algorithm', in International Conference on Information Computing and Applications, pp. 232–241.

Yoon, B & Chang, H 2014, 'Potentialities of data-driven nonparametric regression in urban signalized traffic flow forecasting', *Journal of Transportation Engineering*, vol. 140, no. 7, pp. 04014027.

Yu, B, Song, X, Guan, F, Yang, Z & Yao, B 2016, 'k-Nearest neighbor model for multiple-time-step prediction of short-term traffic condition', *Journal of Transportation Engineering*, vol. 142, no. 6, pp. 04016018.

Zadeh, LA 1965, 'Fuzzy sets', *Information and Control*, vol. 8, no. 3, pp. 338–353.

Zaki, JF, Ali-Eldin, A, Hussein, SE, Saraya, SF & Areed, FF 2019, 'Traffic congestion prediction based on Hidden Markov Models and contrast measure', *Ain Shams Engineering Journal*, vol. 11, no. 3, pp. 535–551.

Zhan, C, Gan, A & Hadi, M 2011, 'Prediction of lane clearance time of freeway incidents using the M5P tree algorithm', *IEEE Transactions on Intelligent Transportation Systems*, vol. 12, no. 4, pp. 1549–1557.

Zhang, GP 2003, 'Time series forecasting using a hybrid ARIMA and neural network model', *Neurocomputing*, vol. 50, pp. 159–175.

Zhang, J, Zheng, Y & Qi, D 2017, 'Deep spatio-temporal residual networks for citywide crowd flows prediction', in Thirty-First AAAI Conference on Artificial Intelligence. San Francisco, California.

Zhang, M 2016, 'Real-time traffic flow prediction using augmented reality', Master's thesis, University of Windsor (Canada).

Zhang, Y & Huang, G 2018, 'Traffic flow prediction model based on deep belief network and genetic algorithm', *IET Intelligent Transport Systems*, vol. 12, no. 6, pp. 533–541.

Zhao, Z, Chen, W, Wu, X, Chen, PC & Liu, J 2017, 'LSTM network: A deep learning approach for short-term traffic forecast', *IET Intelligent Transport Systems*, vol. 11, no. 2, pp. 68–75.

Zheng, B, Sayin, MO, Lin, C-W, Shiraishi, S & Zhu, Q 2017, 'Timing and security analysis of VANET-based intelligent transportation systems', in IEEE/ACM International Conference on Computer-Aided Design (ICCAD), pp. 984–991. Irvine, California.

Zheng, Z & Su, D 2014, 'Short-term traffic volume forecasting: A k-nearest neighbor approach enhanced by constrained linearly sewing principle component algorithm', *Transportation Research Part C: Emerging Technologies*, vol. 43, pp. 143–157.

Zhu, L & Jin, S 2011, 'Speed estimation with single loop detector using typical effective vehicle length', in International Conference on Multimedia Technology, pp. 4096–4099. Hangzhou, China.

Index